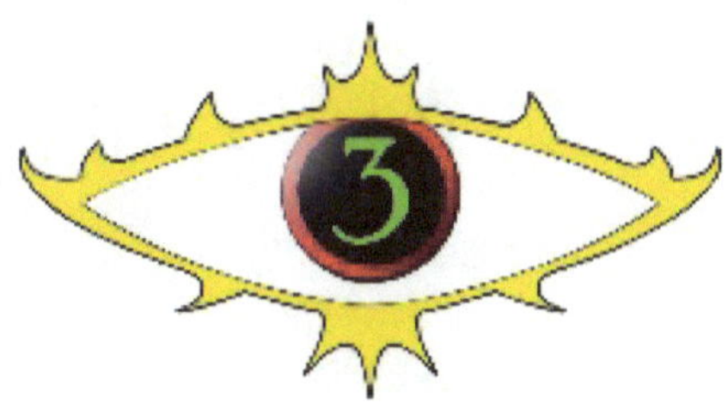

Copyright © 2024 Taurean Washington

All rights reserved. No part of this book may be reproduced
or used in any manner without the prior written permission of the copyright owner,
except for the use of brief quotations in a book review.

To request permissions, contact the publisher at taureanwashingtonart@gmail.com.

Paperback: 979-8-8691-5197-1

Edited by Taurean Washington
Cover art by Taurean Washington
Layout by Taurean Washington
Photographs by Taurean Washington

Taurean Washington Studios LLC
Elkridge, MD 21075

www.taureanwashingtonstudios.com

<u>HALFTIME</u>

30 Years of Select Artworks by Taurean Washington

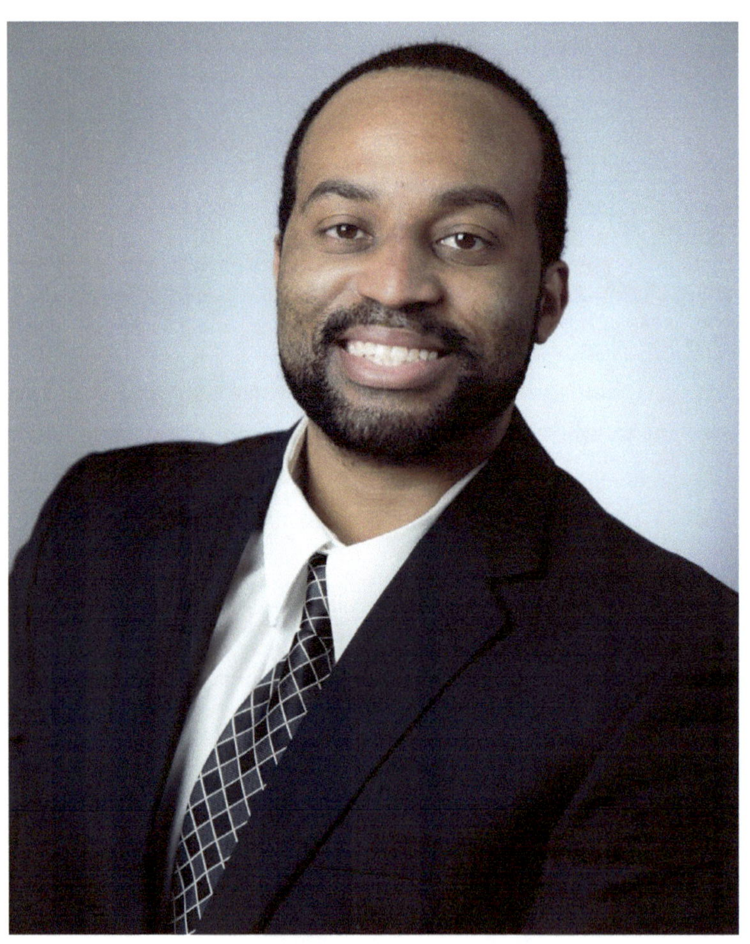

<u>Dedications</u>

GOD *To you I give all the glory. None of this would be possible without you. I am grateful for your grace*

My Wife Tanesha *Thank you so much for your selflessness, unconditional love, the life you give Love you*

My 3 Sons *You make me into a better man. You all are little now but I hope to make you proud Love you*

Lecarolyn "Mama "*I have this warmth of love. I love you and thank you for everything You saved me*

Dena Short *Thank you Mom for giving me life and your sacrifice. Love you*

Reginald Washington *Thank you Pop for planting your seed and allowing for my existence. Love you*

Lamont "Dad" Crosby *You have changed and impacted my life in words I can't even explain. Love you*

Andrea "Mother" Bell *Thank you for always being there form me. Gods got us and the best is coming*

Sandra "Momma San" Rogers *From an asthma attack at 7, staying at your house at 20, till now its Love*

Greg "Mr. Greg" Short *You model great characteristics. Thank you for your continued support*

Aunt Sonja Crosby *The latter part of my life, I want to give to you because of what you gave me Love you*

 "Papa" Hari Crosby *You are my only grandfather. You have a great spirit and I thank you. Love you*

Gran Deb/Uncle Ernest *Thank you for being there with me even back I was at my lowest. Love you both*

Aerial, Ryan, Jazmine, Dakota *Hope in the end, I have modeled being a great brother love you*

Charles Thomas *Thank you bro for believing in me when I didn't! Love always*

Gavin Scott *Thank you bro for modeling what I hope to be as a husband and father! Love always*

Keenan- *Cuz the world isn't ready with what you got coming! You next cuz! Love you fam*

Thearon *Keep your head up and I can't wait to see what God has in store for you to do when you out*

Meyah, Serenity, and Mikayden *Love all 3 of you guys and can't wait to see what you accomplish*

Mike "Sensei E" Eubinag *Your philosophies changed my brainwaves man. Thank you for being a guide*

Wendell Poindexter *You have transitioned to teacher to mentor to Friend and I'm thankful for you*

Dr. Bari You are the sole reason I am as informed as an artist, you gave me the spark. I miss you much

Tamelyn Tucker Worgs Thank you for equipping my mind with Theology and your continued support

Andrea McCluskey Our relationship has grown since your Printmaking class thank you for everything

Dr. Ross Thank you for being my advisor and you helped guide me through an important phase in life

Myrna Day "Mrs. Day" *You fostered my gifts at an early age and you truly helped me bud as a learner*

Extended Porter and Washington Family *Love y'all and hope I represent the fam on both sides!*

<u>FOREWARD</u>

In case you have not heard of me or seen my art by now, my name is Taurean Washington, visual artist and entrepreneur based in Howard County Maryland. This book serves as a life's retrospective with my art up until 2023(1993-2023) which spans 30 years of my practice. Please pay attention to everything that I state in this forward. My words are not to be minced and everything said is intentional because they have a purpose.

What I am about to say is not out of spite, resentment, disgruntlement, or anger. It is my reaction to what is and what has been established from the beginning. Just as Ibram X. Kendi stated, we as African Americans as a whole have been "Stamped from the Beginning". So, it was already pre-determined by society centuries ago that individuals with my same skin tone and ethnicity that I am not intellectually capable to make works of art or to be just as sophisticated or more sophisticated as my white counterparts.

We live in a society that White people are the default. As a result, everything else is "OTHER". If you don't believe me, look at blogs and articles when referring to any artist of color. You will see Black Artists, Asian Artists, Indian Artists, Indigenous Artists, Latino Artists, etc. Have you ever seen an article about White Artists? They just say American Artist or just Artist. But aren't I American? I thought America is a country. Is America a race? I was born and raised in America and according to my ancestry, my family trees is traceable as far back since the 1860s but even then, it would be safe to assume I had family going back to when our people first settled in this country in the 1700s or so. I'm not a history buff but I'm telling me along with my family have been American for quite sometime but for some reason I'm not seen as one.

So next time an interviewer asks me about the great artists today, I will be sure to say that I like "White Artists" such as George Condo, Jeff Koons, Mr. Brainwash, and Banksy. Until you stop calling me a black artist, I will continue to say "White Artists" or artists of European descent. By calling me a Black Artist, you are indirectly calling me the N-Word. So, what are you really saying by calling me a "Black Artist"? Art is universal. Put Art first because that puts us all on the same level. By putting black or any other racial identifier, you are already boxing myself and other artists to the "Other" category on purpose so you can set us aside from the default which is "White". I am aware of what is taking place and will no longer stand for this anymore.

 Although I am excited that Artists of African American descent is getting attention, I question the sustainability of it and if it is merely a trend. I am a big fan of contemporaries such as Amy Sherald, Rashid Johnson, Titus Kaphar, Kehinde Wiley, Hank Willis Thomas, Nina chanel Abney, and Mickalene Thomas.

I have my Bachelor's Degree in Studio Art from Hood College. Even though I wasn't accepted in Grad School, I am now happy how my development of an artist panned out. Going to Grad School wouldn't have already meant that I would have been "discovered" by museums and institutions. We live in a society that rely on Institutions and gatekeepers in order to attain prestige, validation, marquee, and platforms. I refuse to engage or do that anymore.

I am not waiting for Taschen to publish me, I am not going to be discouraged or upset I am not on the New York Times Best Seller List, and I am not going to even worry if I ever have my art hanging on a museum wall. As a kid that was my dream to have my art in a museum. But after seeing this system for how it works, the agendas, and politics of the personnel selected to run the programing behind the institutions, I respectfully do not care and know God is going to get me where I need to be and that is right here with you who is reading this book.

This book is called Halftime because to me art is a sport. It is my Basketball; it is my solo sport that I train every day for. Like Malcolm Gladwell, I put in my 10,000 hours. The first half of this game from 1993-2023 I took a lot of time understanding the other team and they are really dominating the game. I put a few points on the board but I am trailing behind a bit. But right now, the coach who I refer to as God has implemented in me how to strategize and run new plays. So, stay tuned for this next quarter. Big things are coming and I am coming for that championship. I am building a dynasty and my art is going to change the world!

If you have a dream do not let anyone or even society deter you from your mission. It wasn't meant for a boy like born on Riverside Drive in Fort Worth Texas to be where I am today. But God will use me to continue to defy the odds. In this lifetime that I am alive, God is taking me to the Naismith Hall of Fame!

Thank you to all who have supported my life and career thus far. The art filled in these pages reflects events, ideas, and emotions I have witnessed or felt over the past 30 years. Take from it as you wish. I hope that you enjoy.

Thank you for your support and God Bless,

Taurean Washington

Aka The Artrepreneur

Aka In the Future will give Jeff Bezos and Elon Musk a run for their money

Aka The founder of Art-Hop (movement I started in 2008 will soon be mainstream)

Aka The next best thing since sliced bread

Aka Going hard in the paint no Waka Flocka

Aka The Artmamba (rest in power Kobe)

Aka Soon to be the Greatest Artist of All time (just watch)

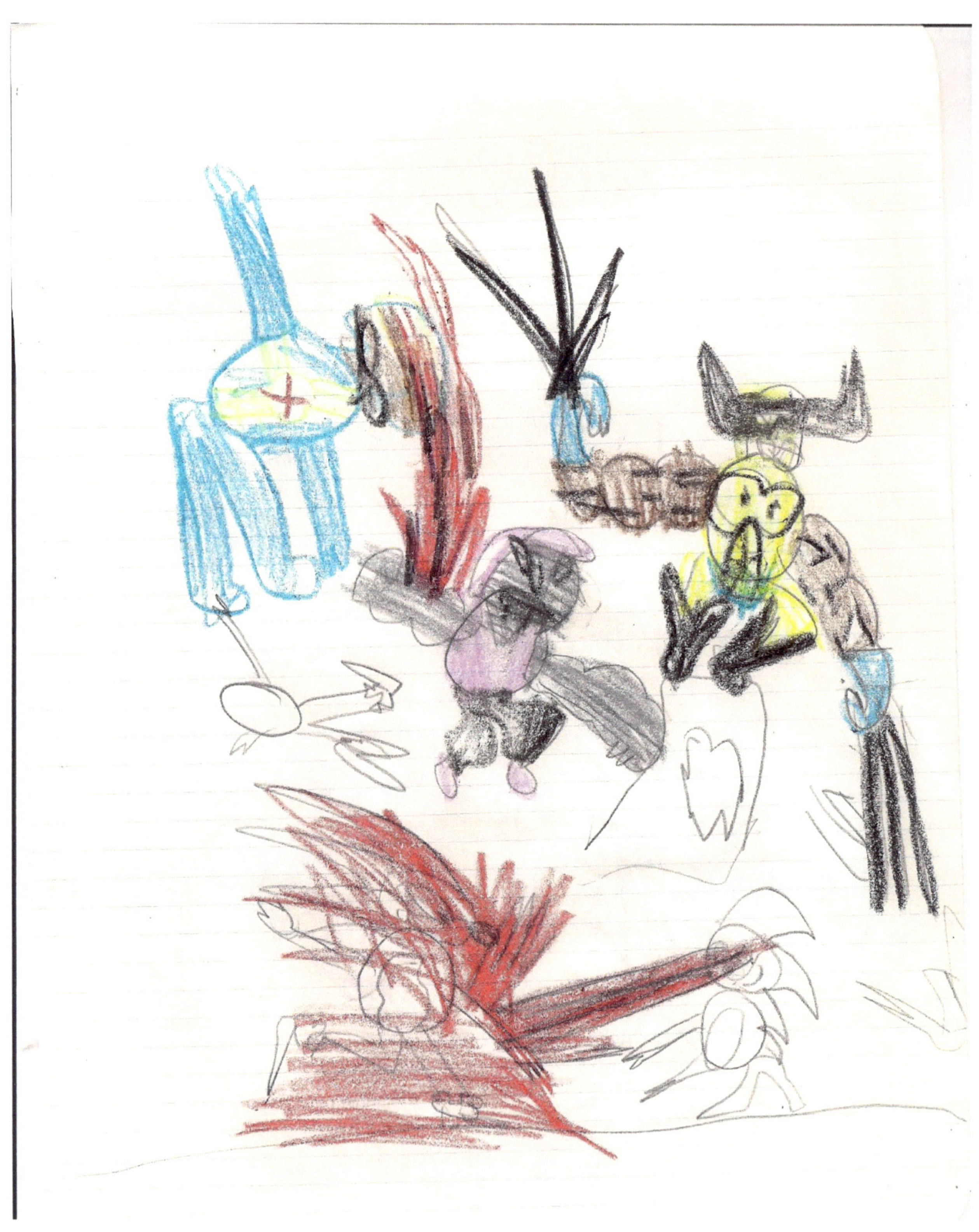

"X-Men #1" **(1993)**

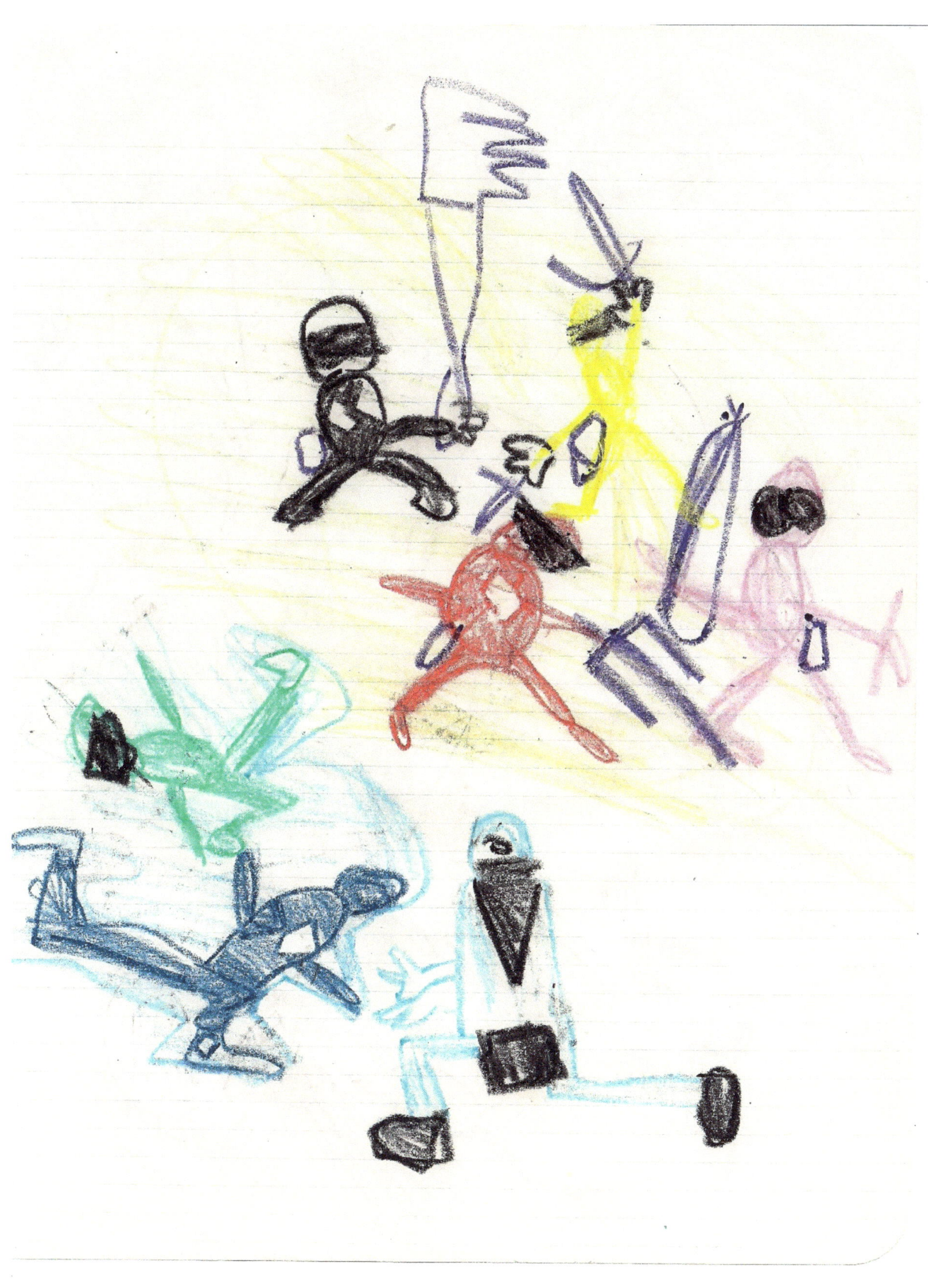

"Power Rangers" **(1993)**

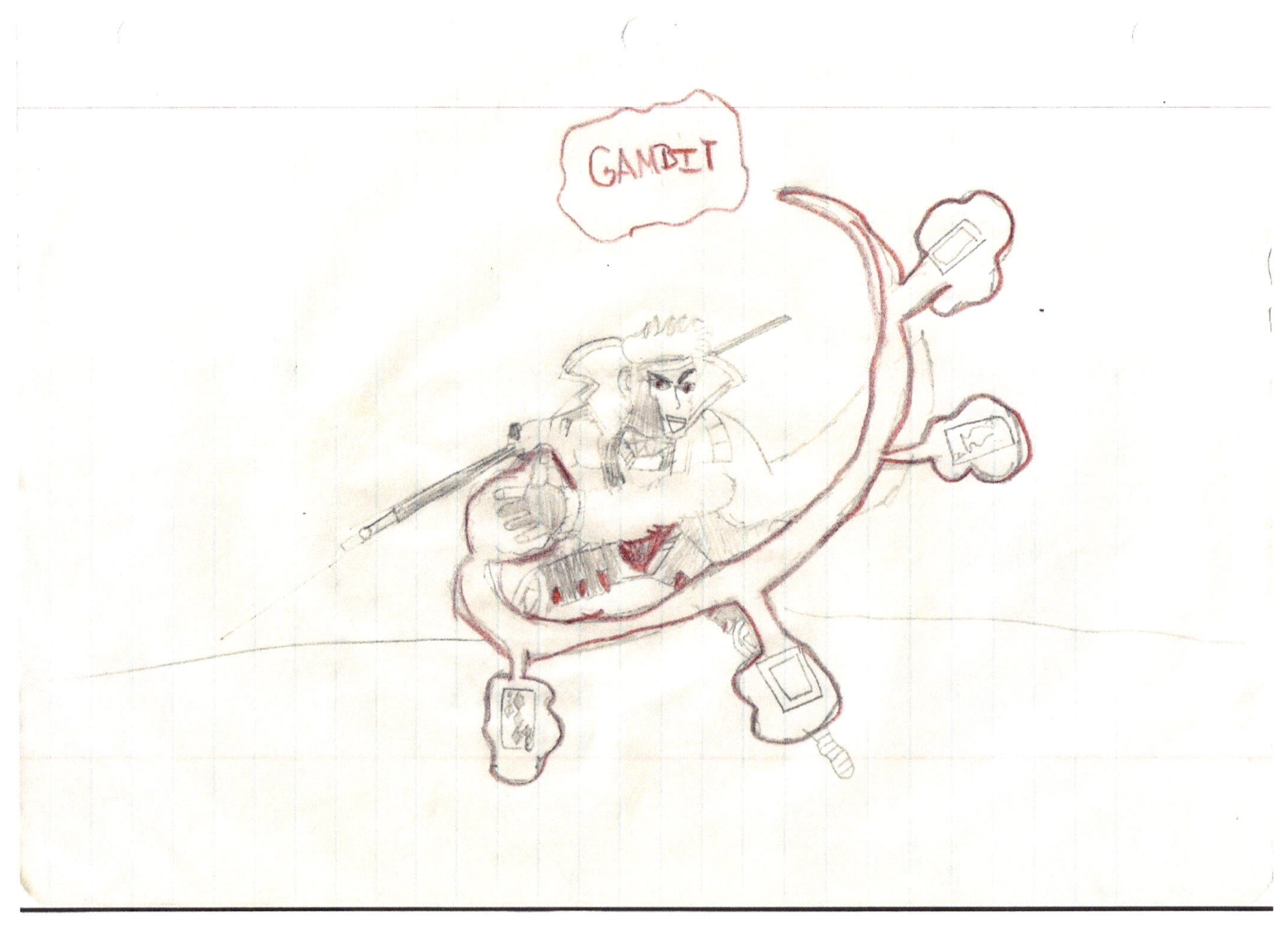

"Gambit" **(1994)**

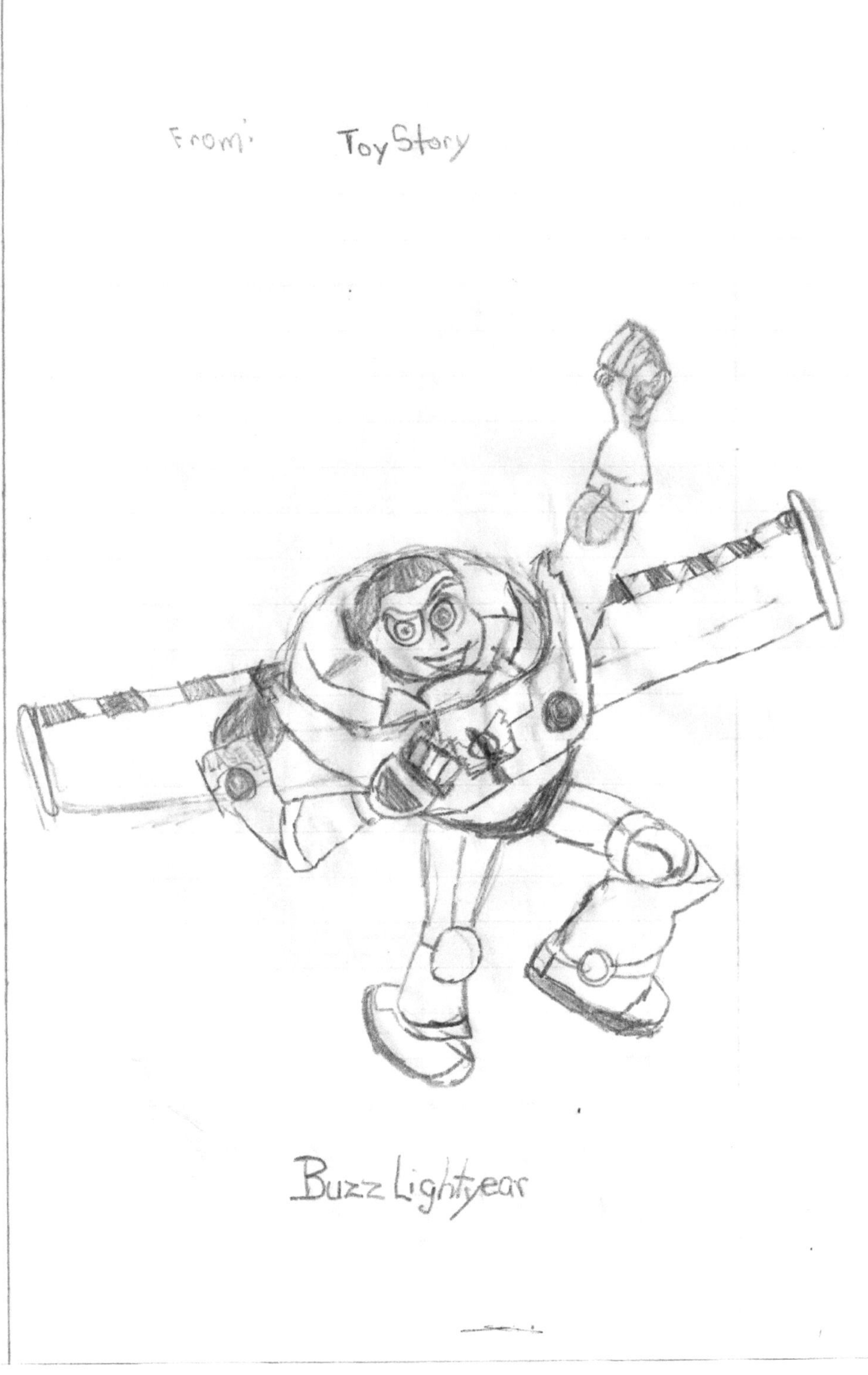

"Buzz Lightyear" **(1994)**

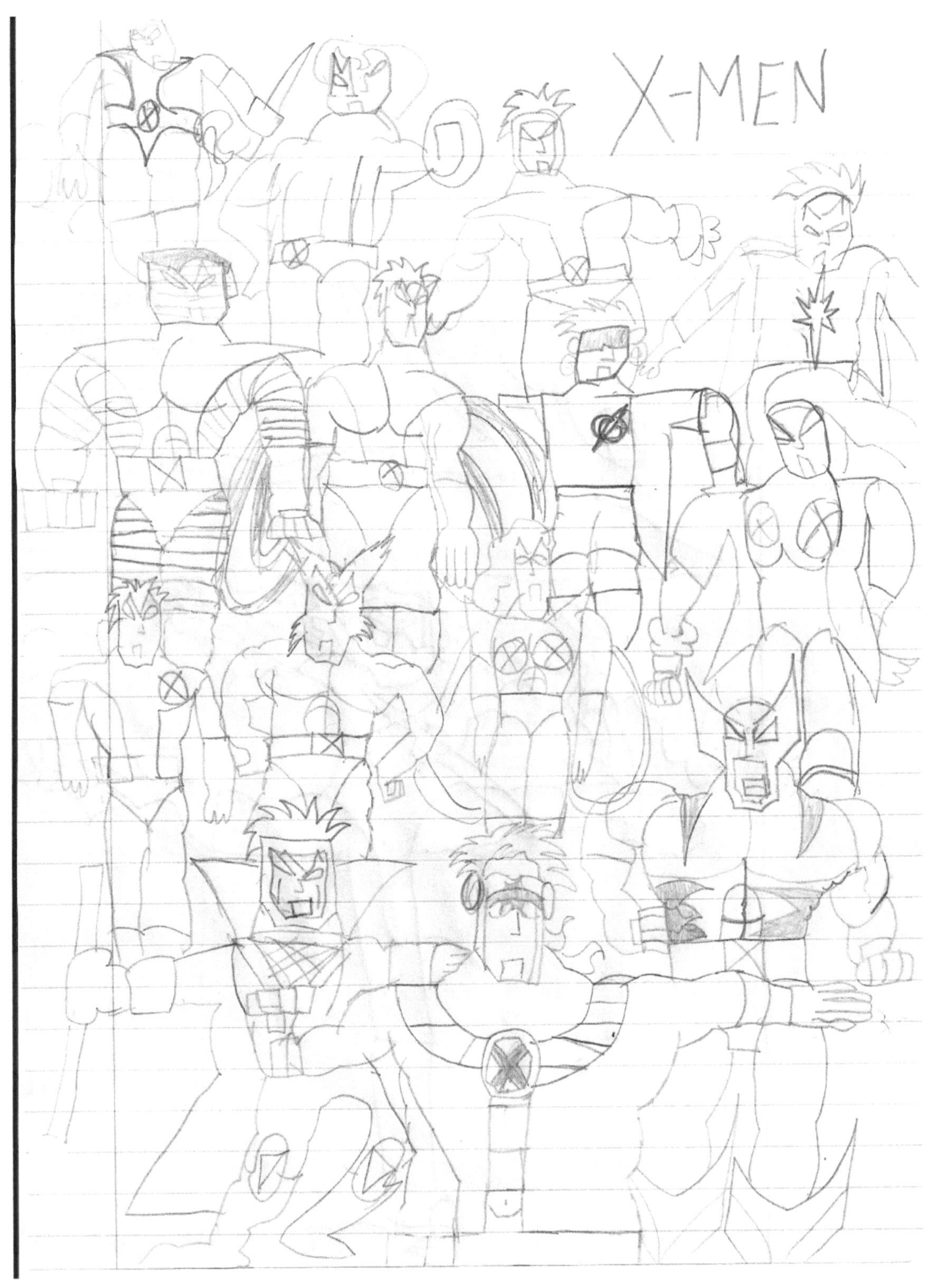

"X-Men #2" **(1995)**

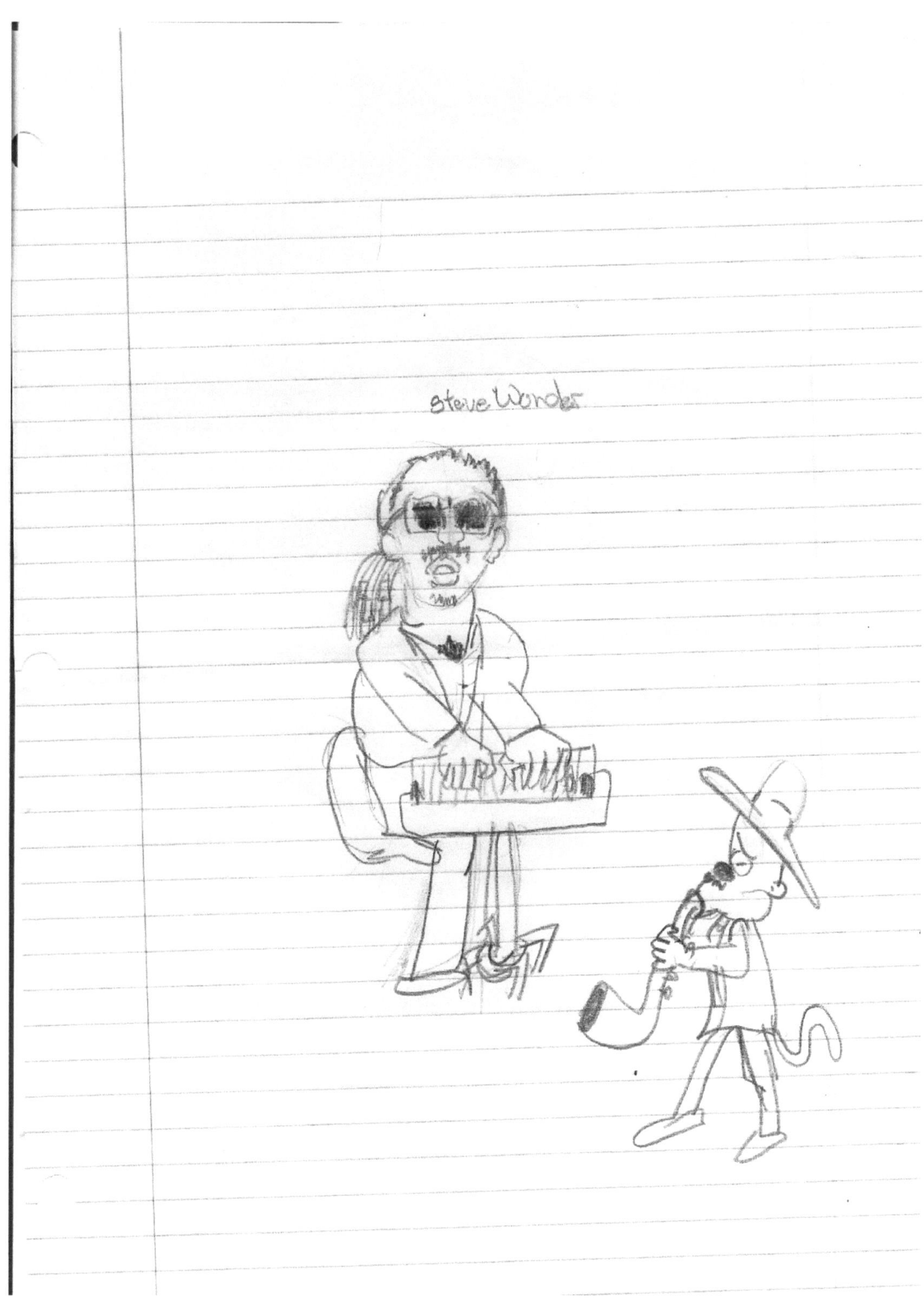

"Stevie Wonder" **(1996)**

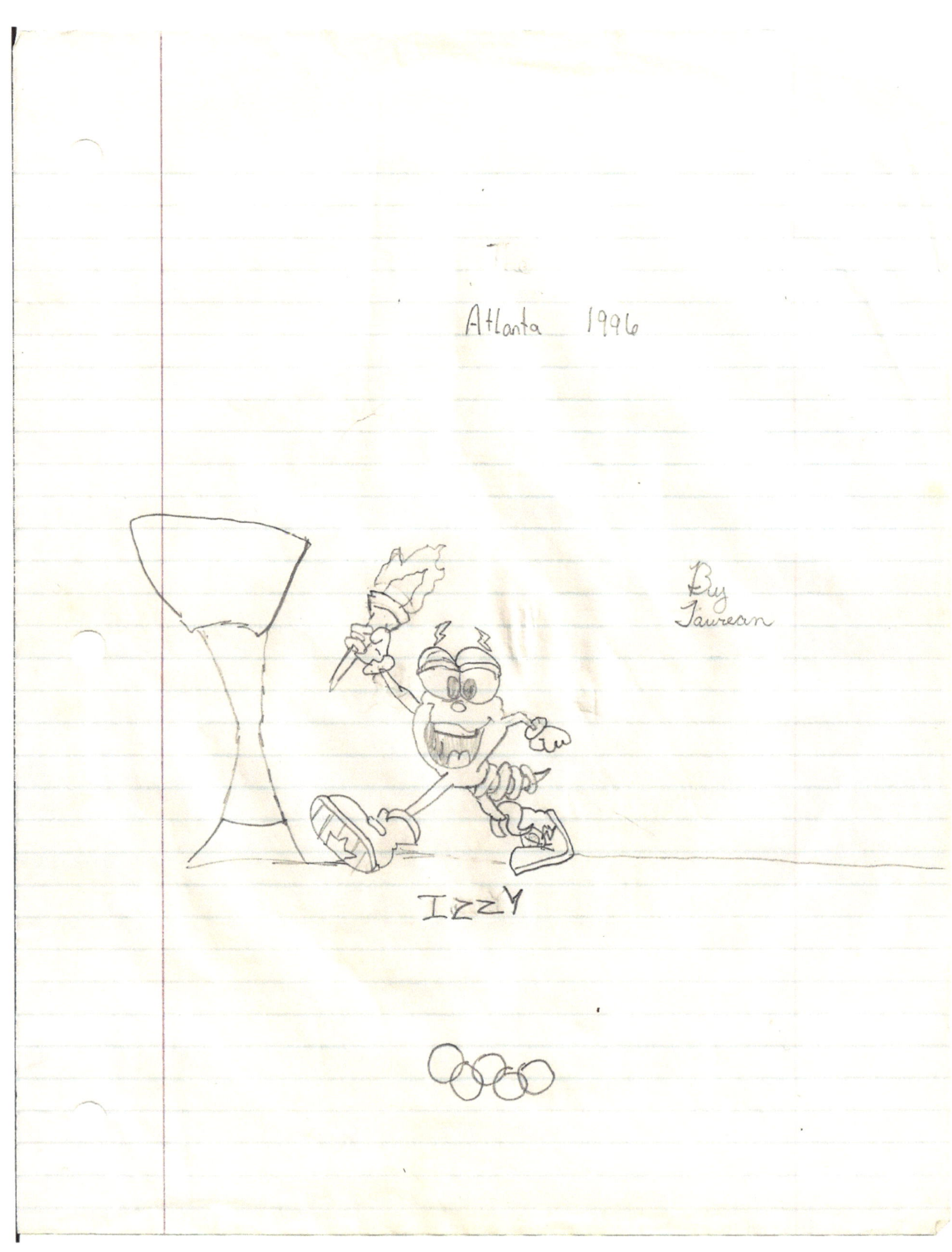

"1996 Olympics" **(1996)**

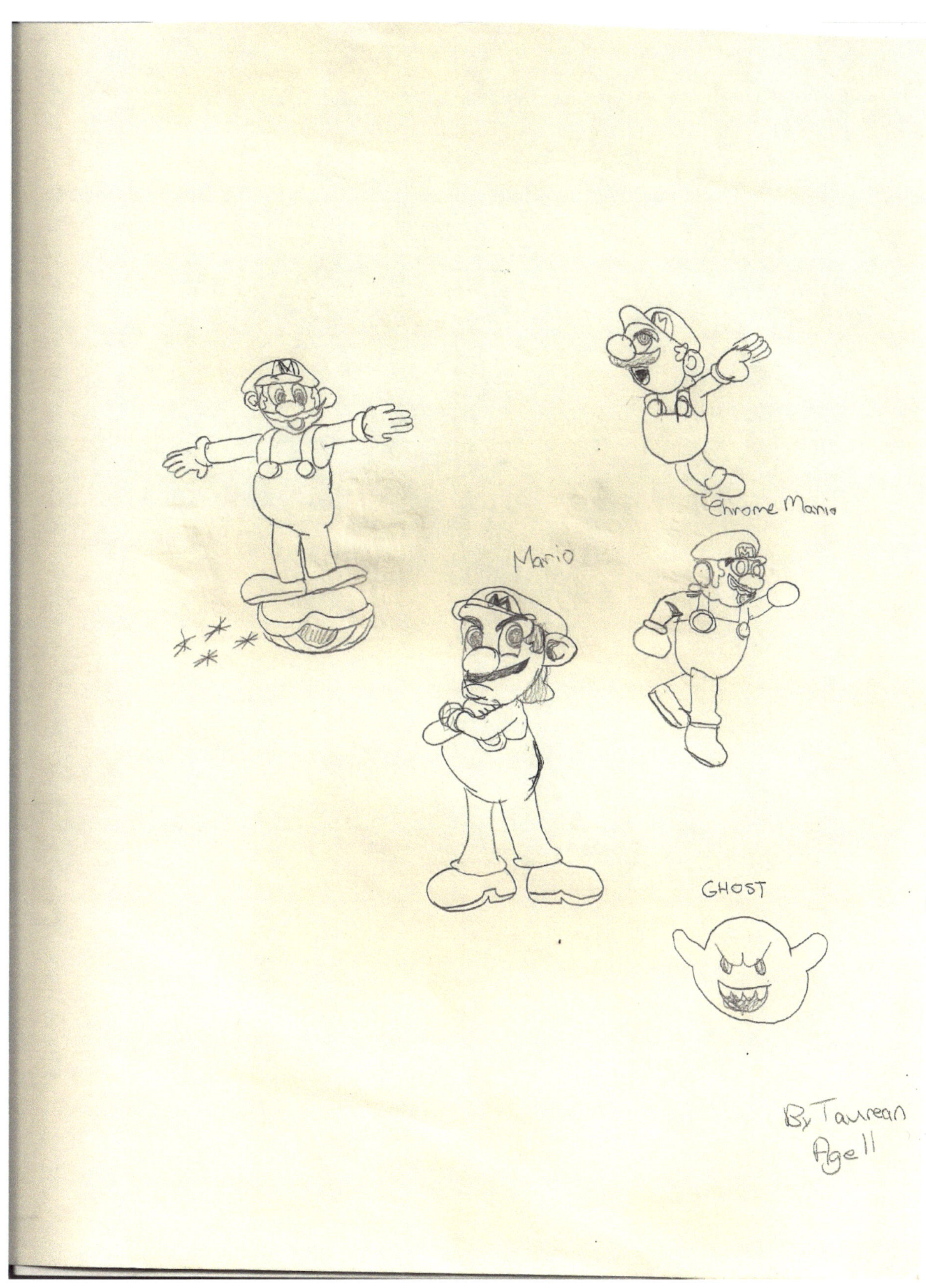

"Mario Universe" **(1997)**

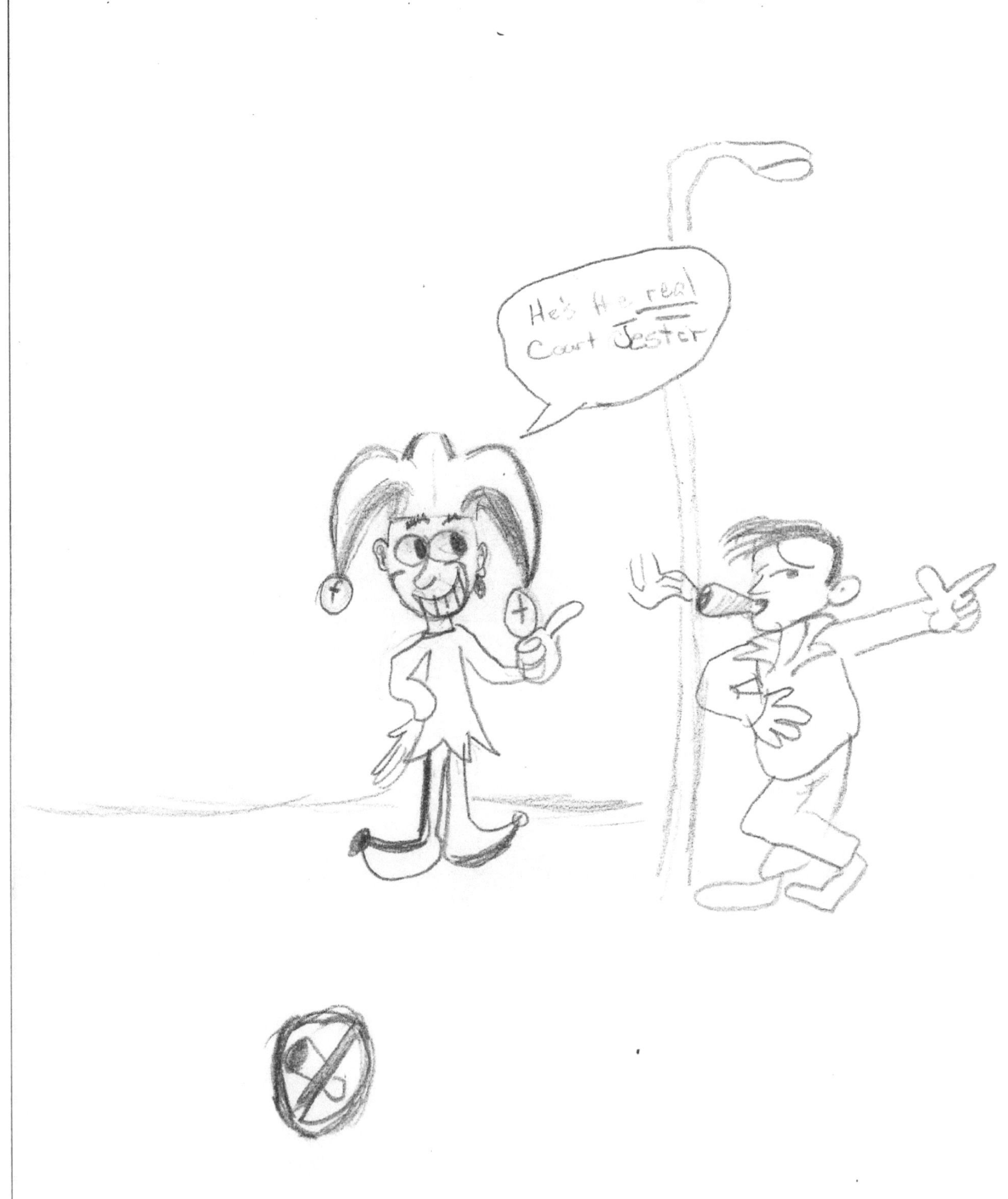

"Smoking Ad" **(1998)**

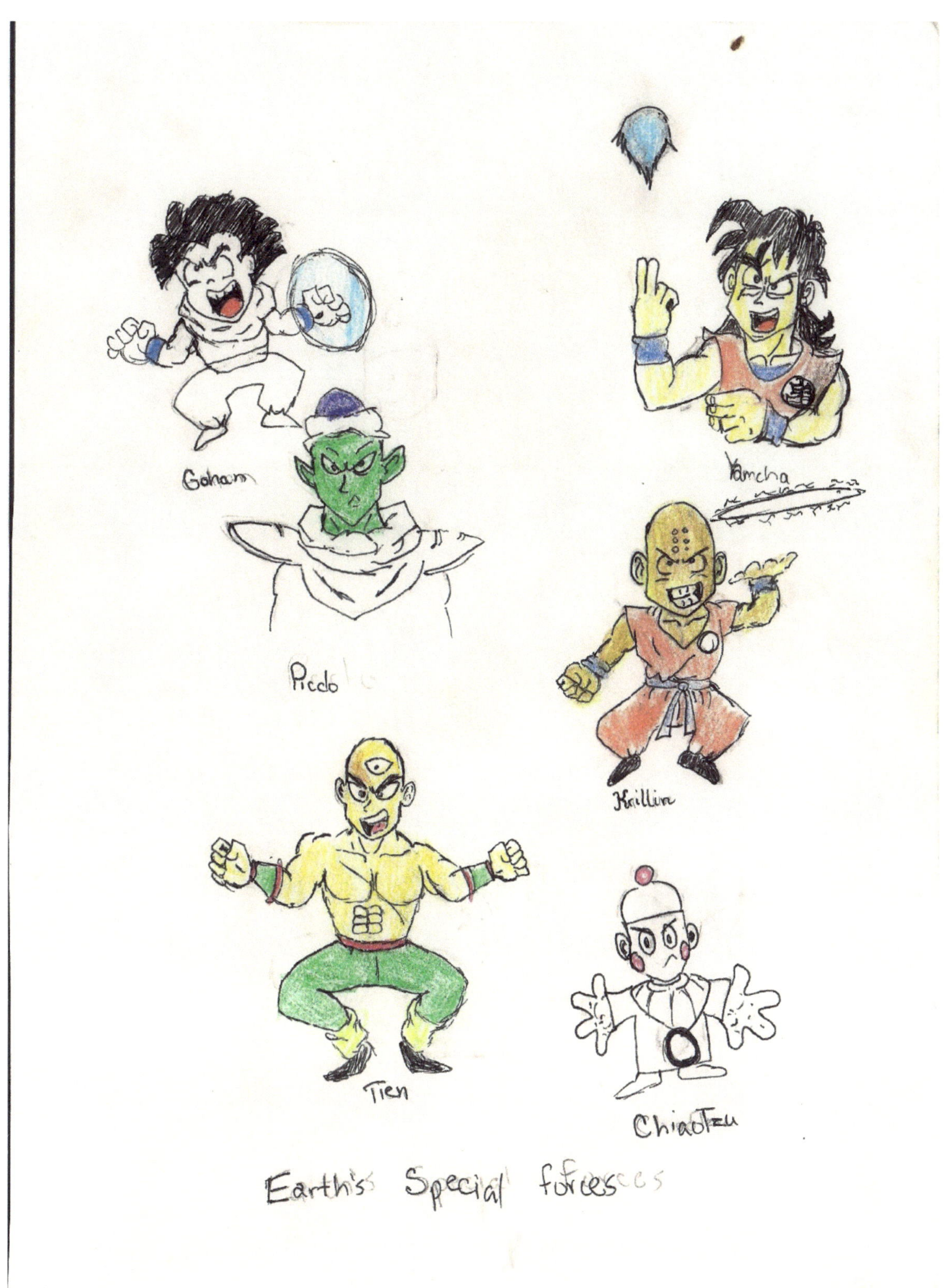

"DBZ Universe" **(1999)**

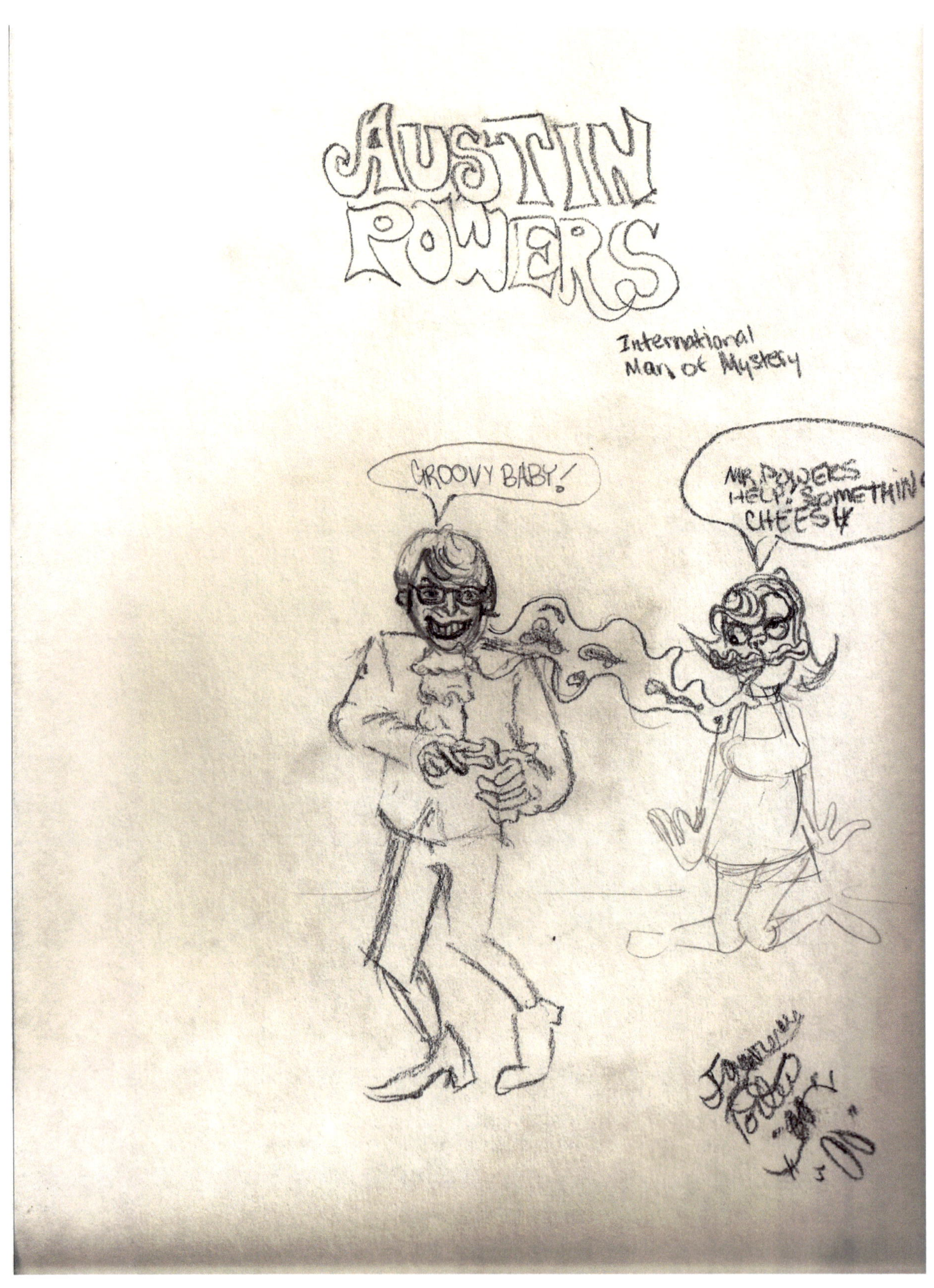

"Austin Powers" **(2000)**

I AM GLAD TO BE BLESSED WITH ALL
THESE MATERIALS TO EXPRESS MY ARTISTIC THOUGHTS. I WON'T FORGET YAS.
I ♡ YOU. GOD IS THE FIRST TO THANK FOR THIS (WITHOUT
HIM WE WOULDN'T BE HERE. SECOND, I WANT TO
THANK MY PARENTS FOR RAISING ME UP TO THE
PRESENT. MY AMBITION IS TO SOMEDAY BE
AN ANIMATOR AND FOLLOW THE FOOTSTEPS OF
CHARLES SCHULZ, WALT DISNEY, DAV PILKEY, BILL
BRUCE BLITZ, AND MANY COUNTLESS OTHERS (
NOT TO MENTION Picasso, Van Gogh, Di Vinci,
Michalangelo, Raphael, Donatello. . . . .

In THE FUTURE, I WANT TO EXCEED
IN EDUCATION AND LATER MAYBE HAVE A FAMILY
AS LONG AS GOD IS BY MY SIDE, THE DEVIL'S
TEMPTATIONS and EVIL WON'T STAND A CHANCE
GOD BLESS

BY
TAUREAN
PORTER
Mar - 11

"Note to Self in Sketchbook" **(2000)**

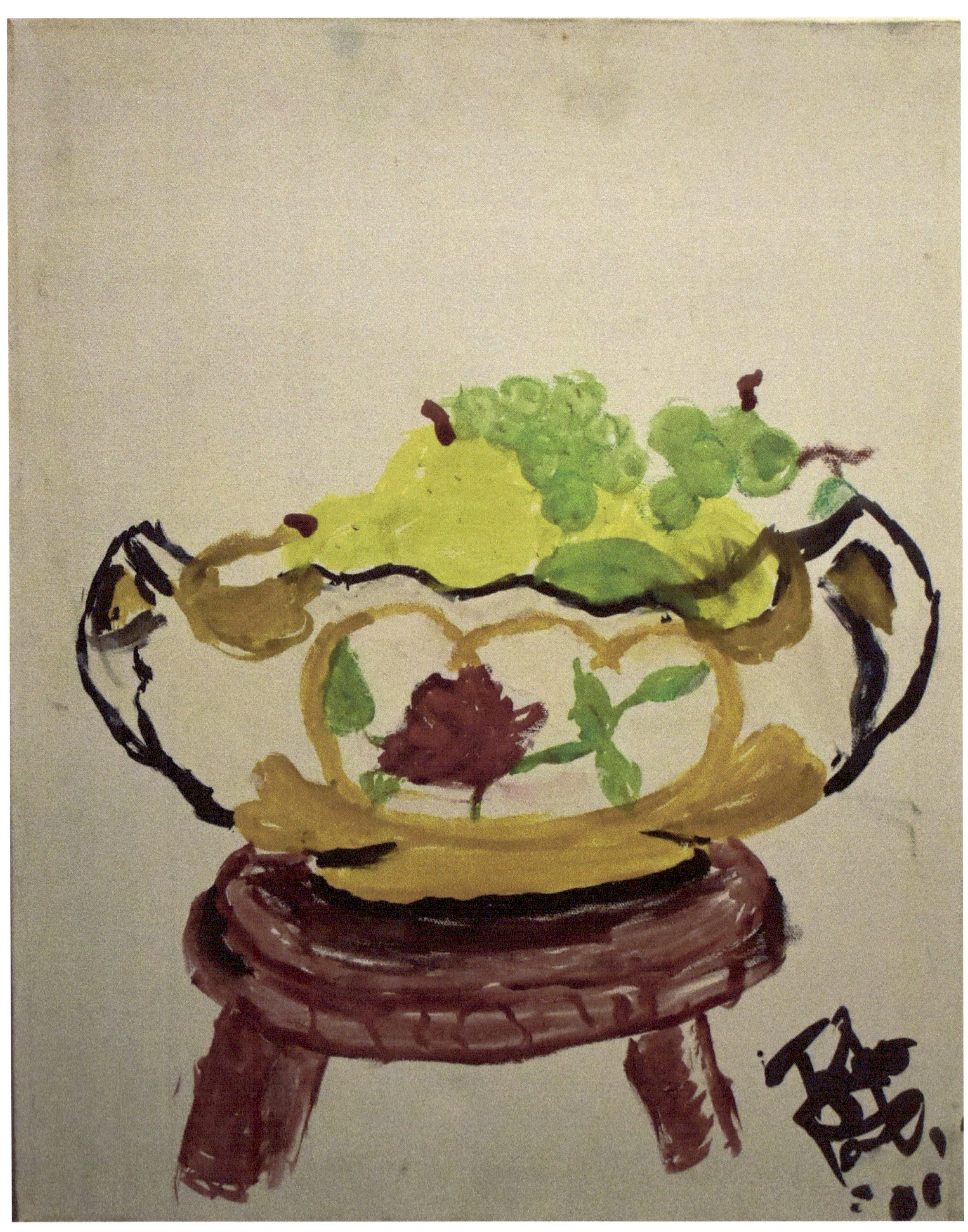

"My First Painting" **(2000)**

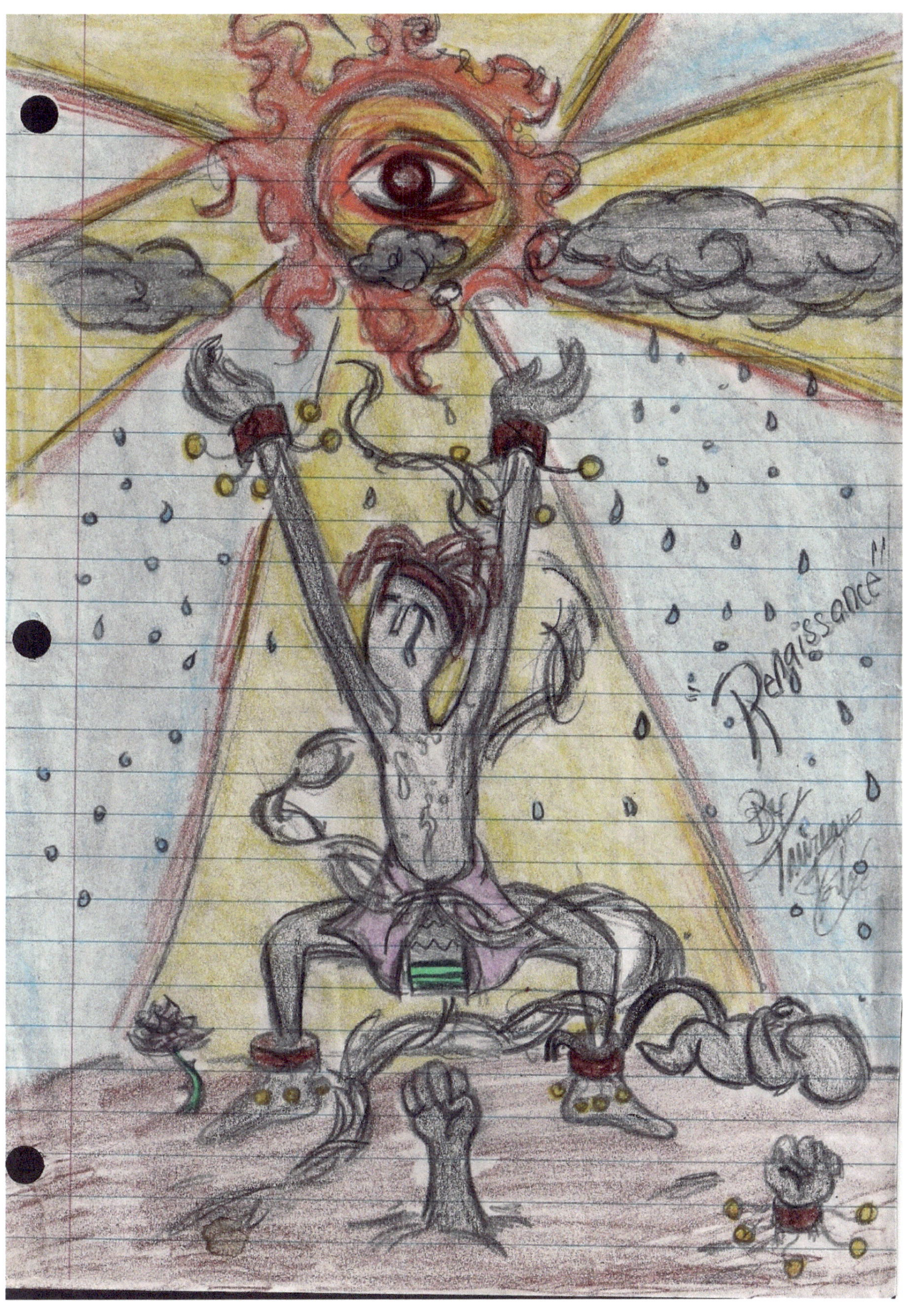

"Renaissance" **(2001)**

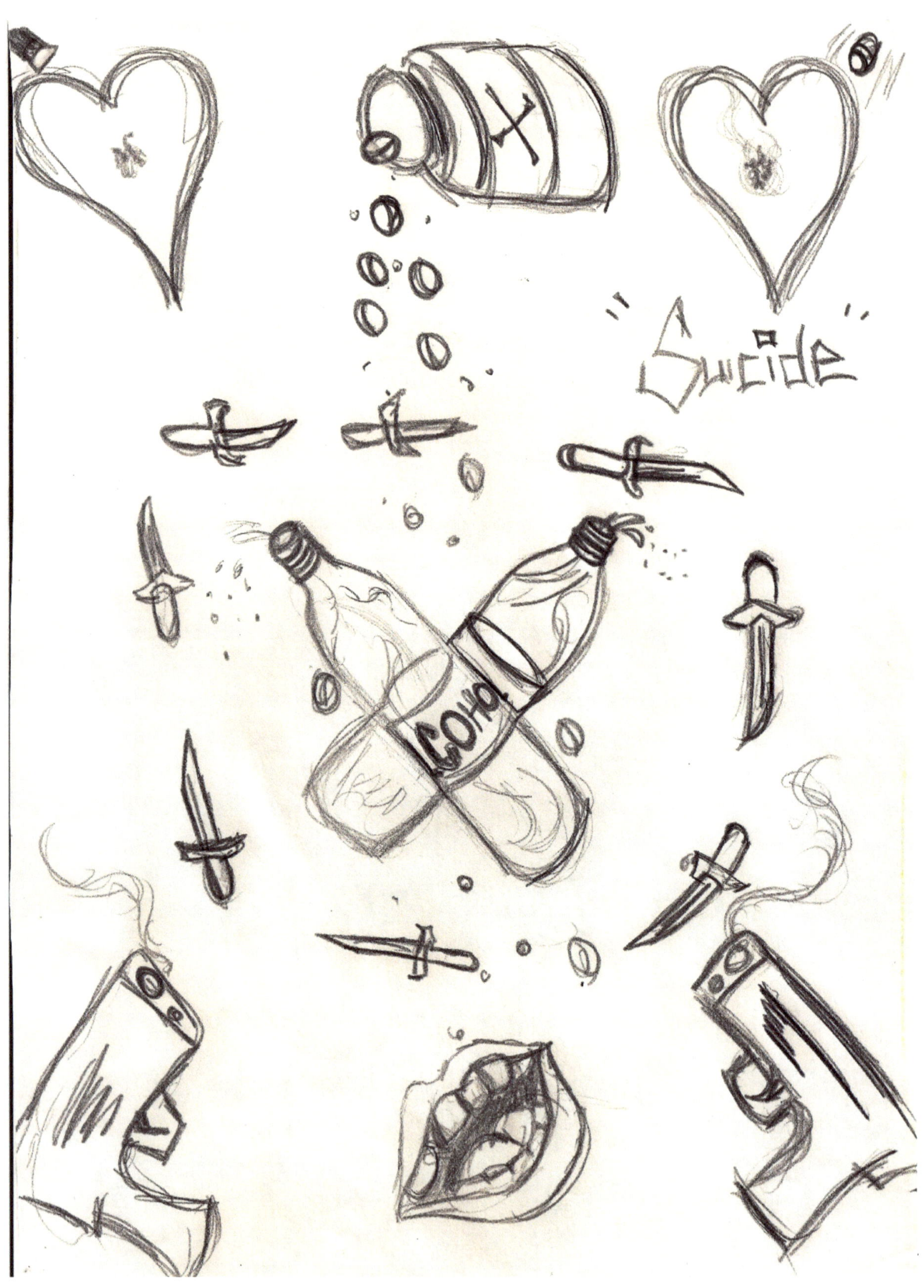

"Suicide" **(2001)**

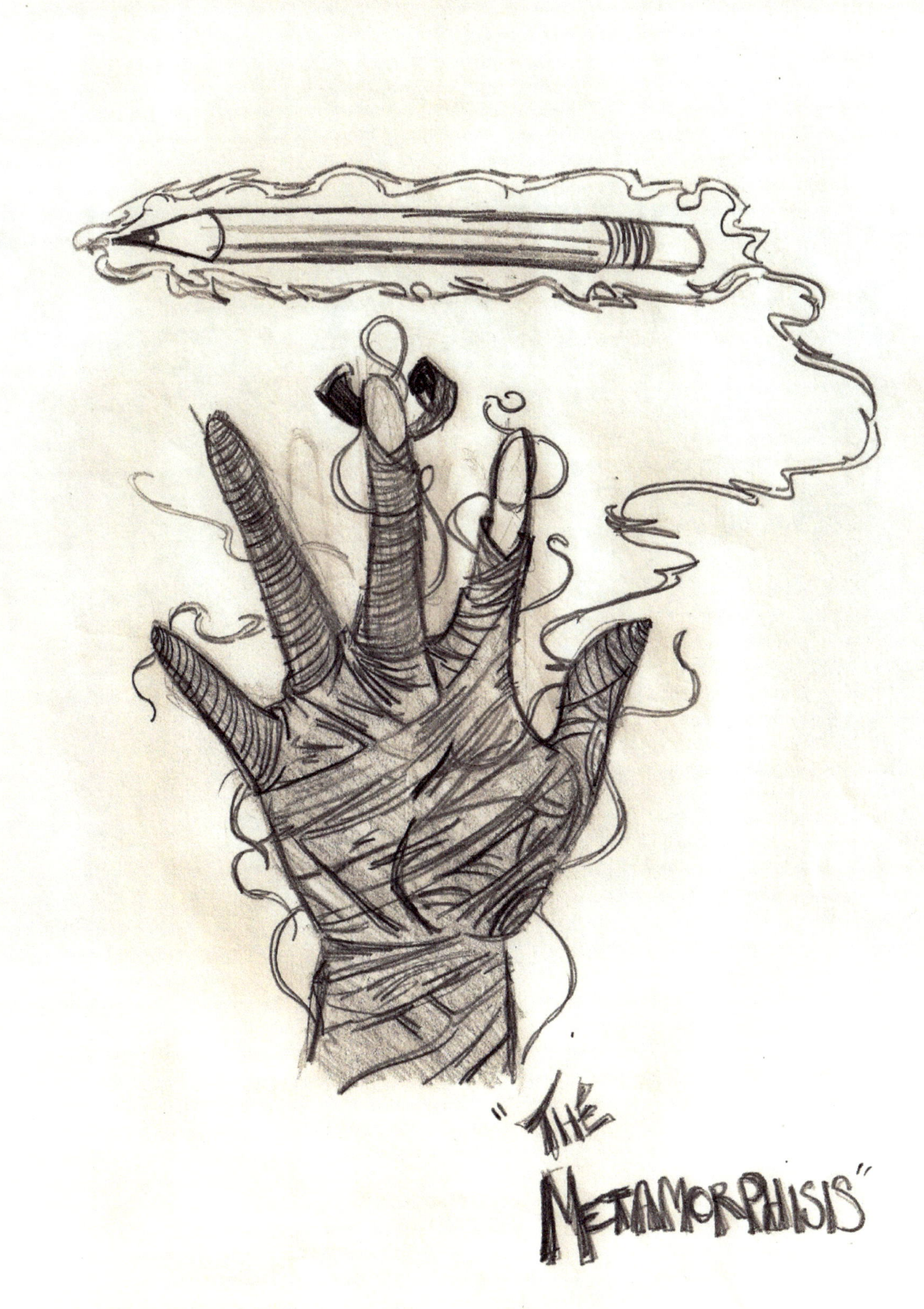

"Metamorphosis" **(2001)**

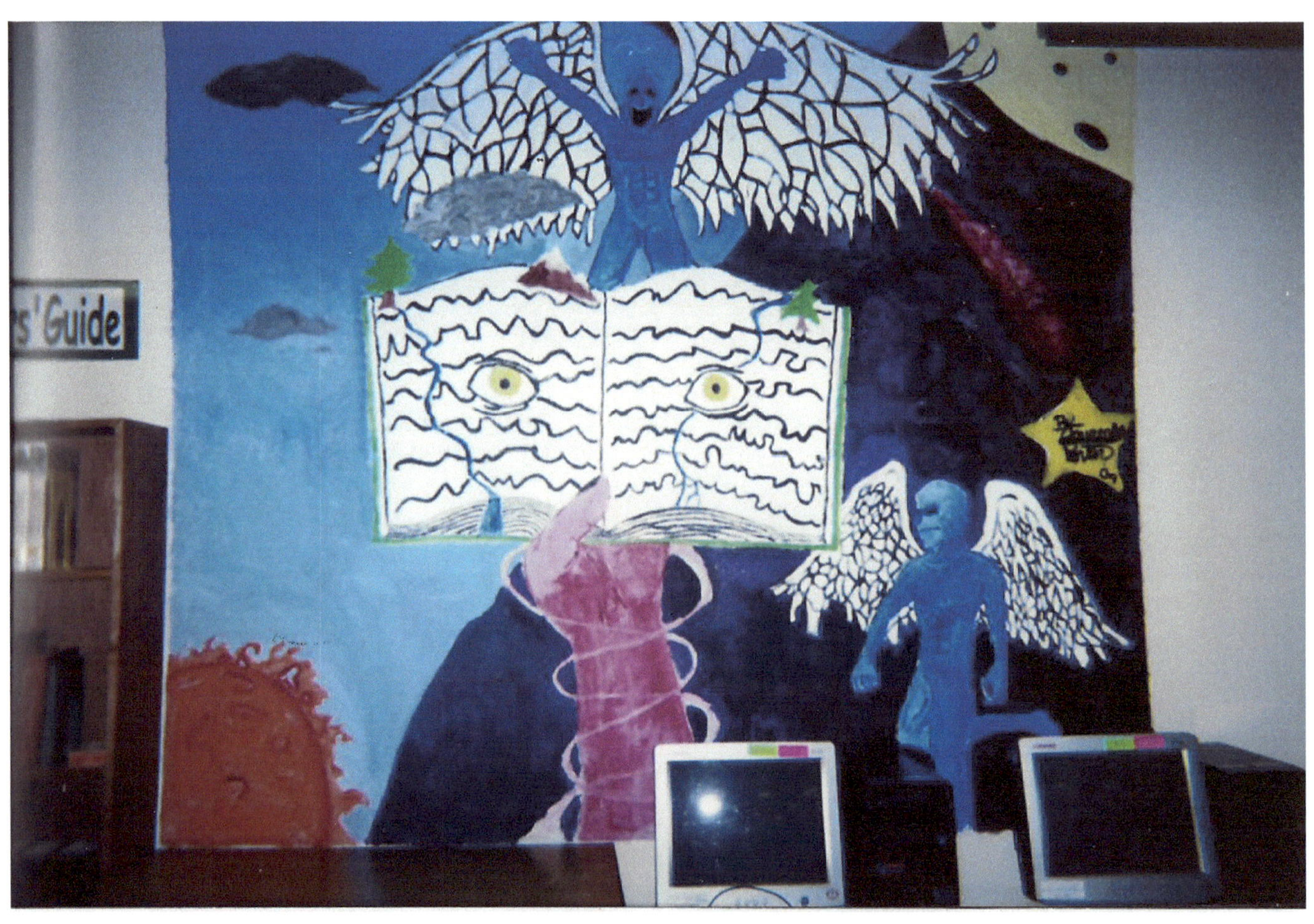

"1st Mural at Aged 15 at Timberline High School in Lacey, WA" **(2001)**

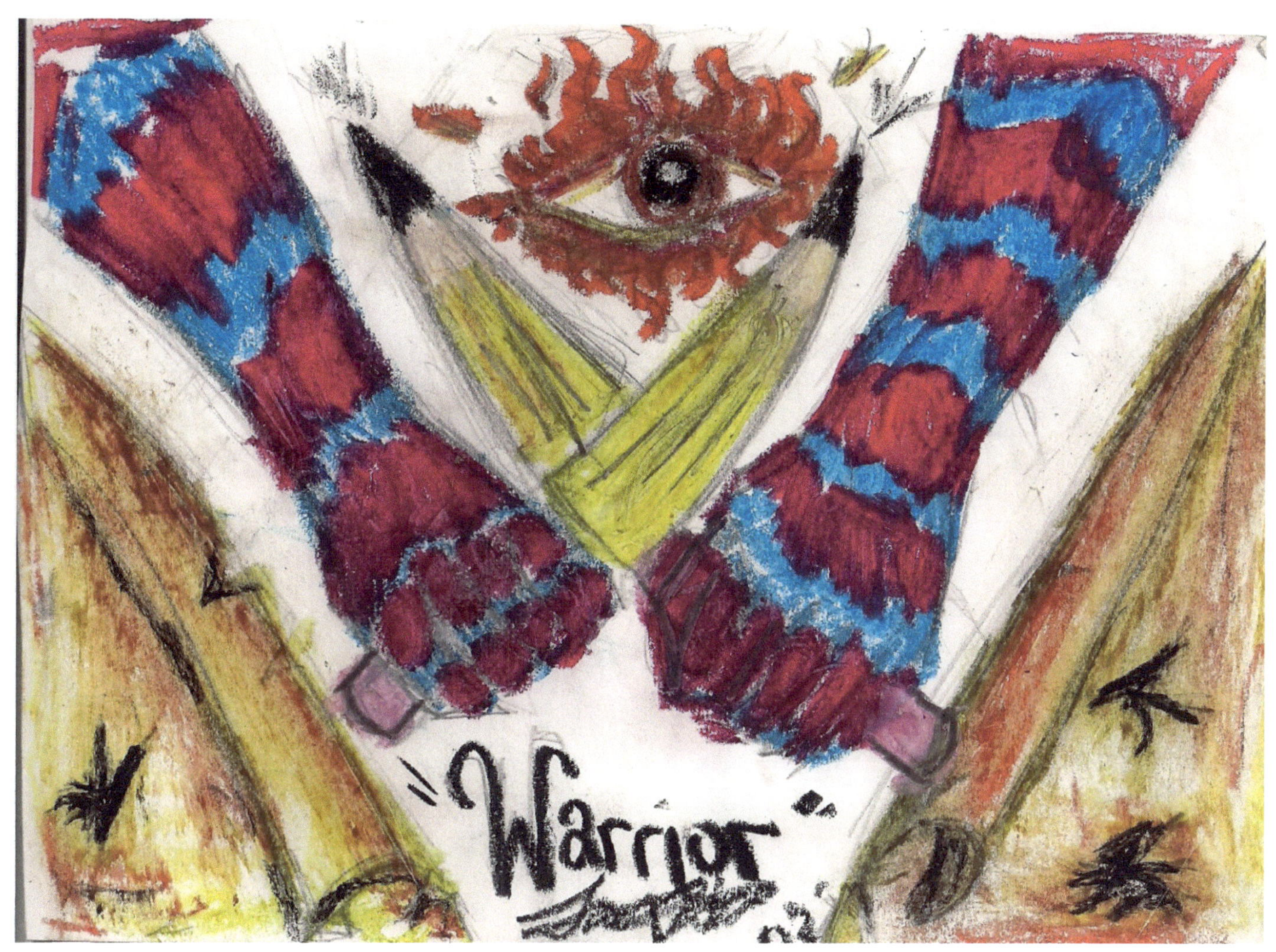

"Warrior" **(2002)**

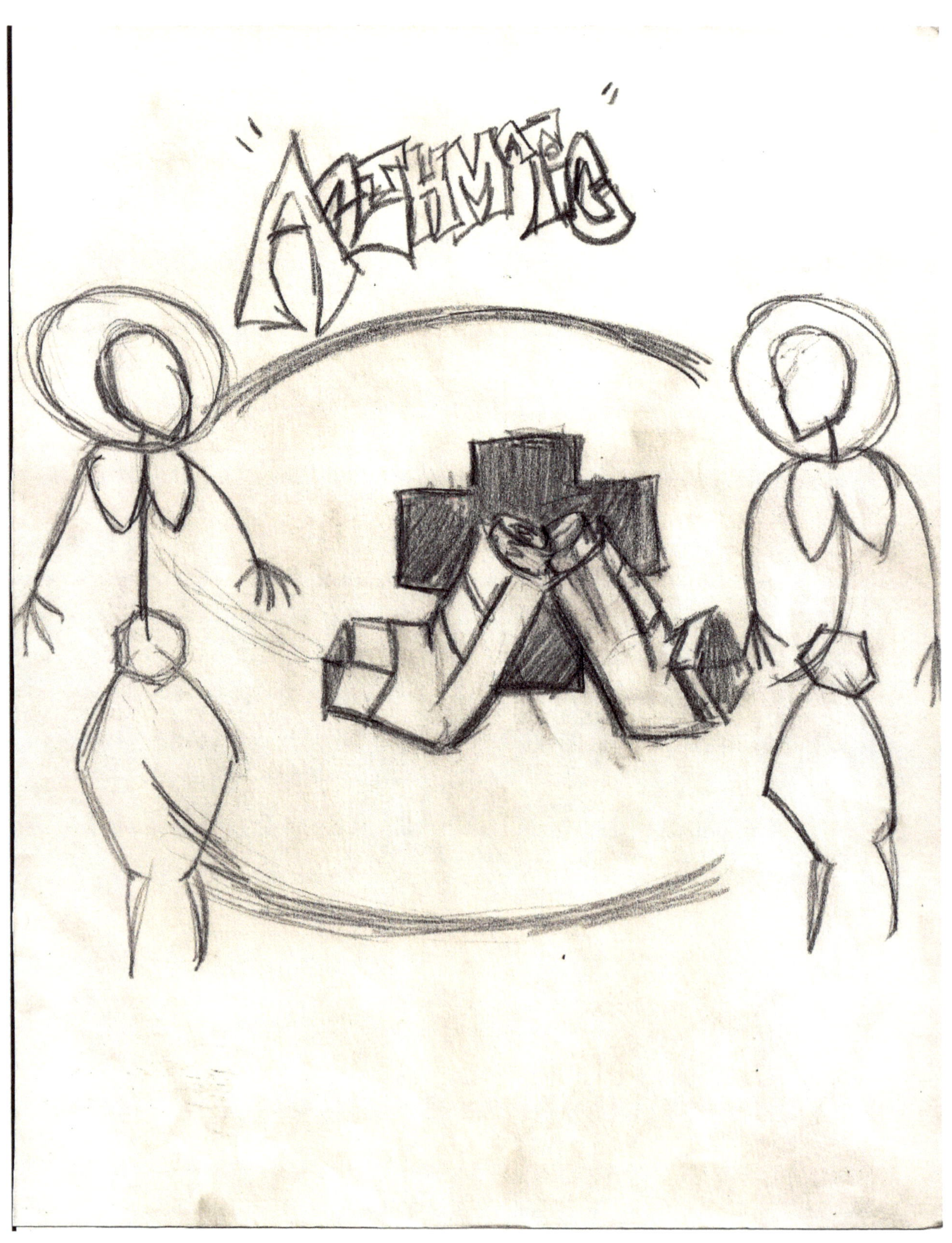

"Asthmatic" **(2002)**

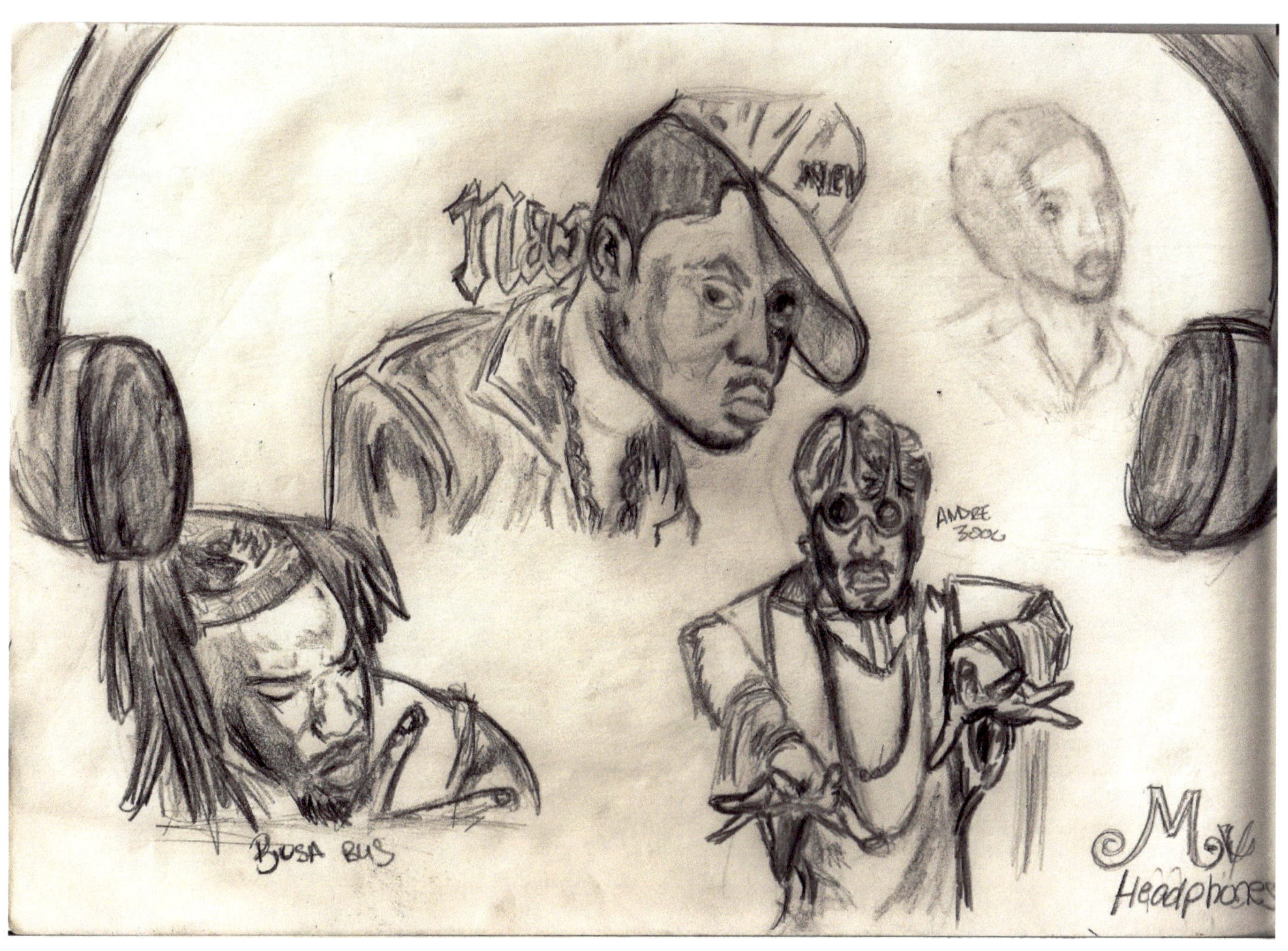

"In My Headphones" **(2002)**

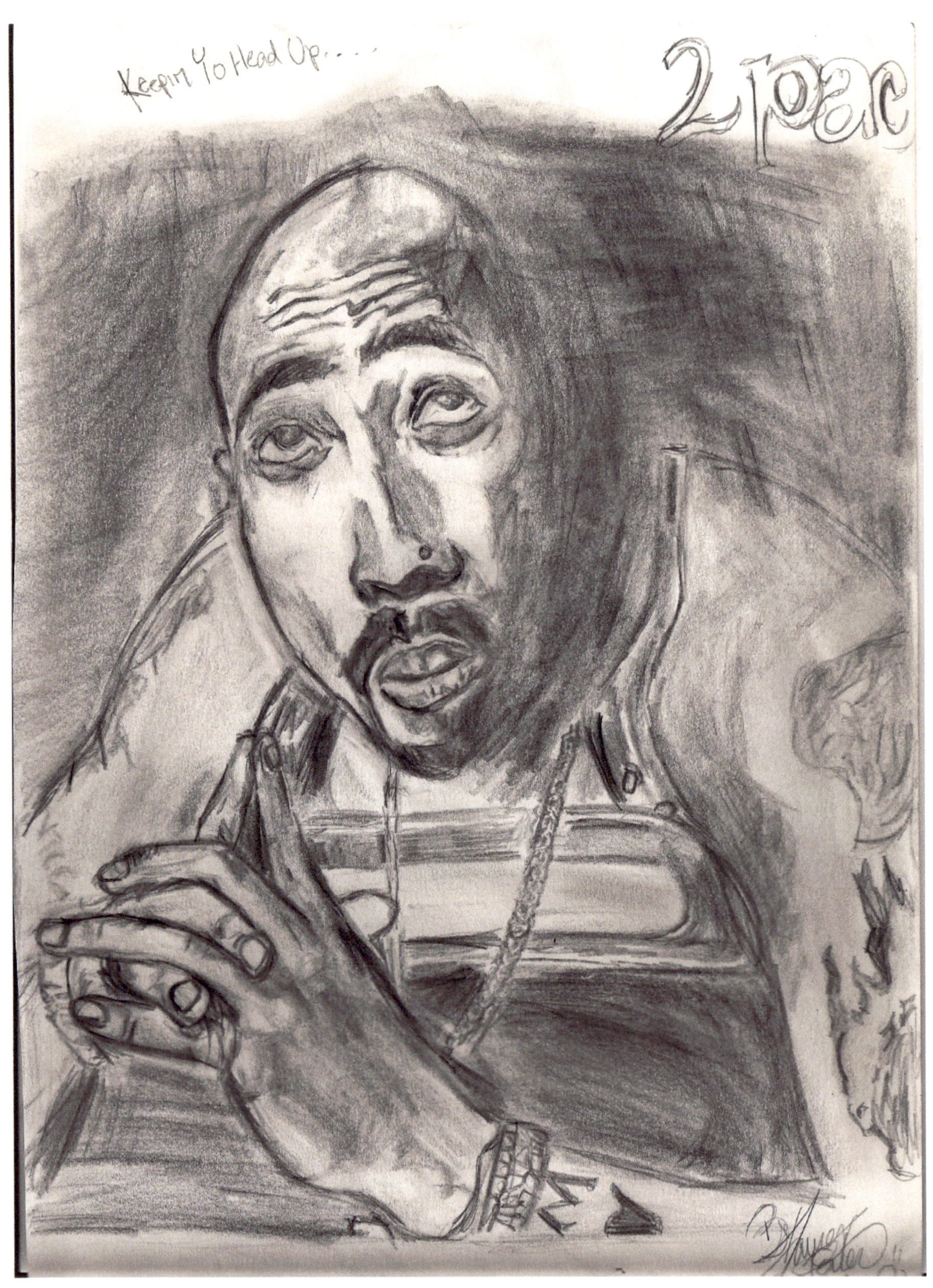

"Pac" **(2002)**

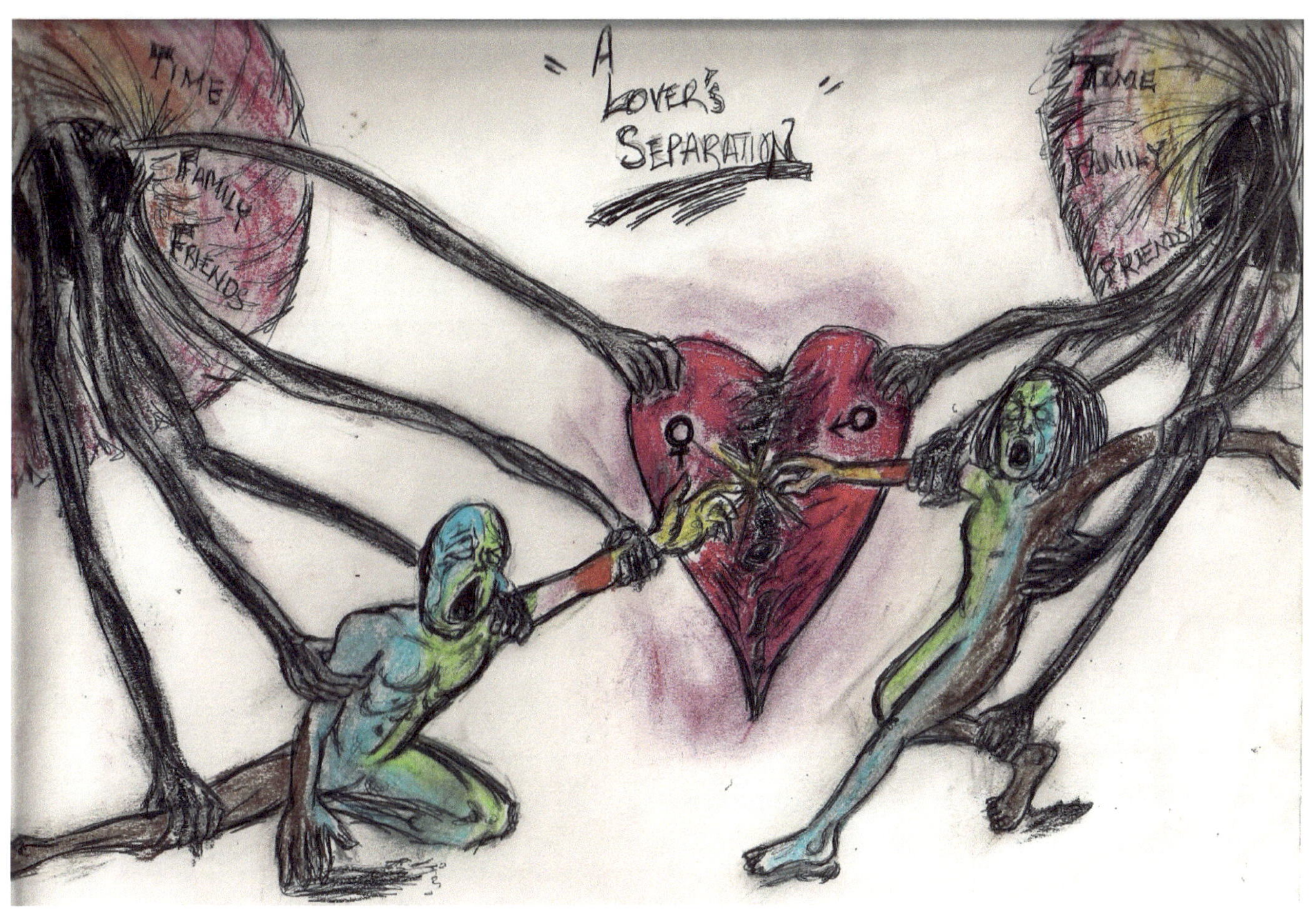

"A Lover's Separation" **(2002)**

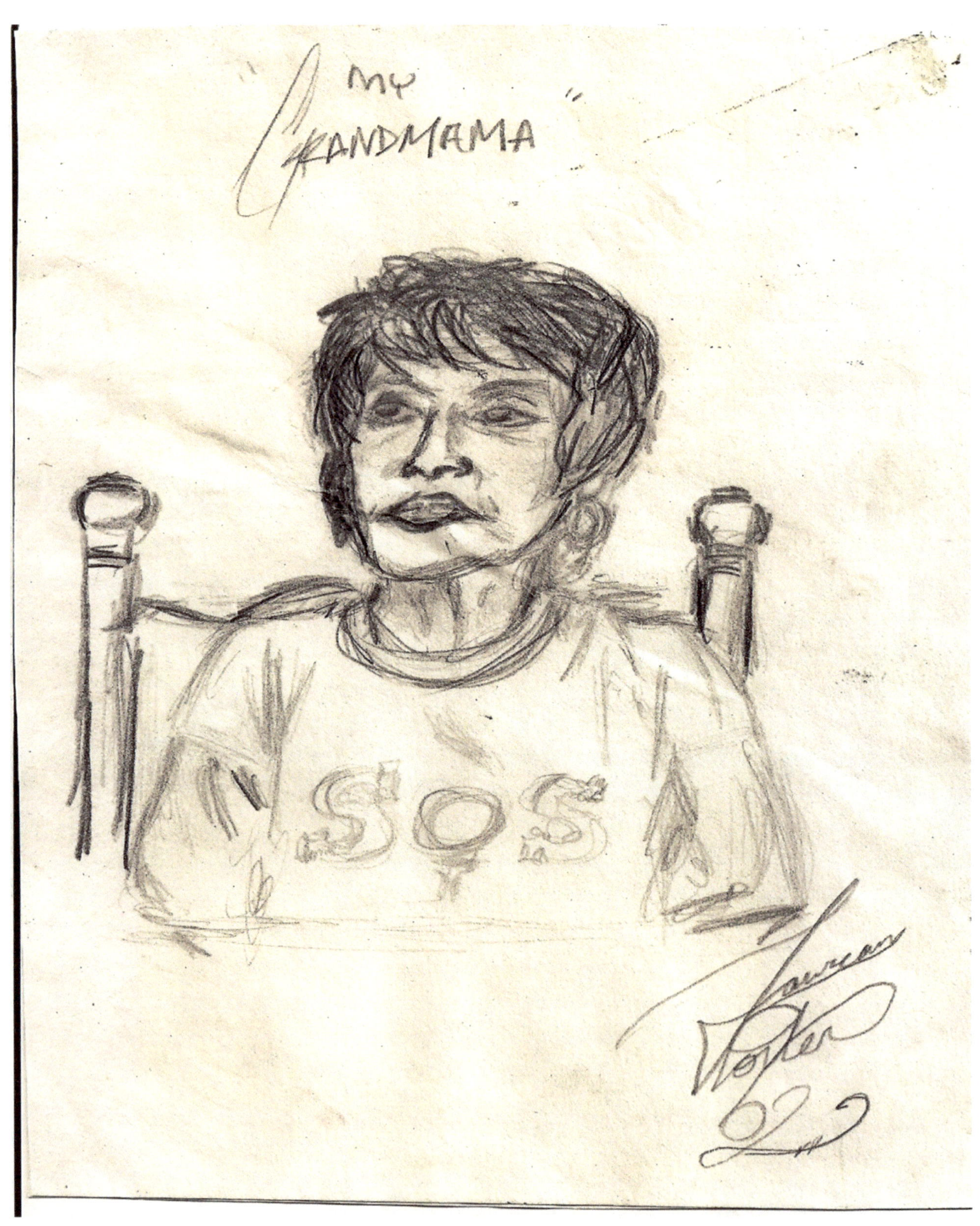

"Mama" **(2002)** *I love you Mama very much. Thank you for everything

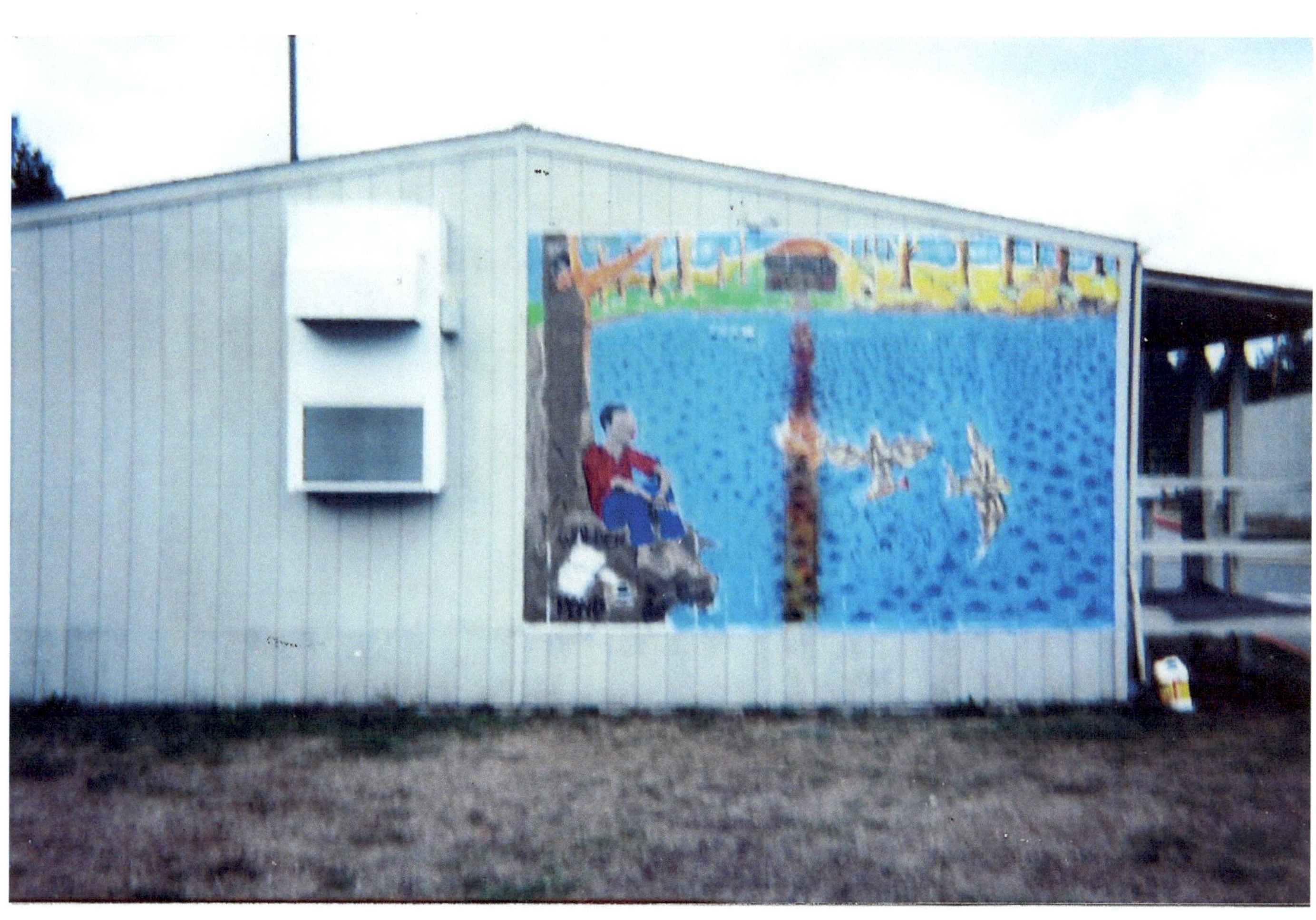

"2nd Mural at age 16 at Timberline High School in Lacey, WA" **(2002)**

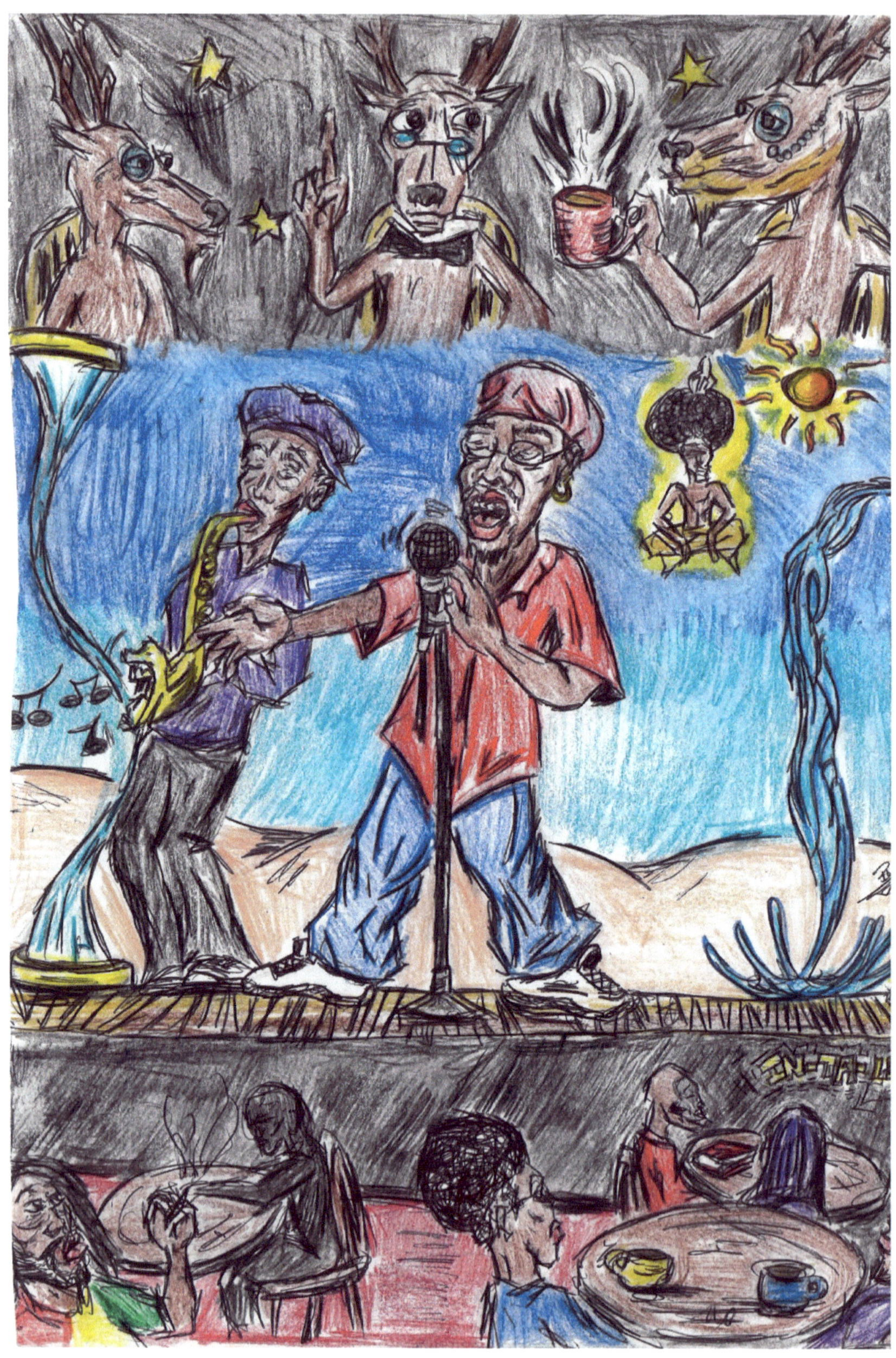

"Floetic" **(2003)**

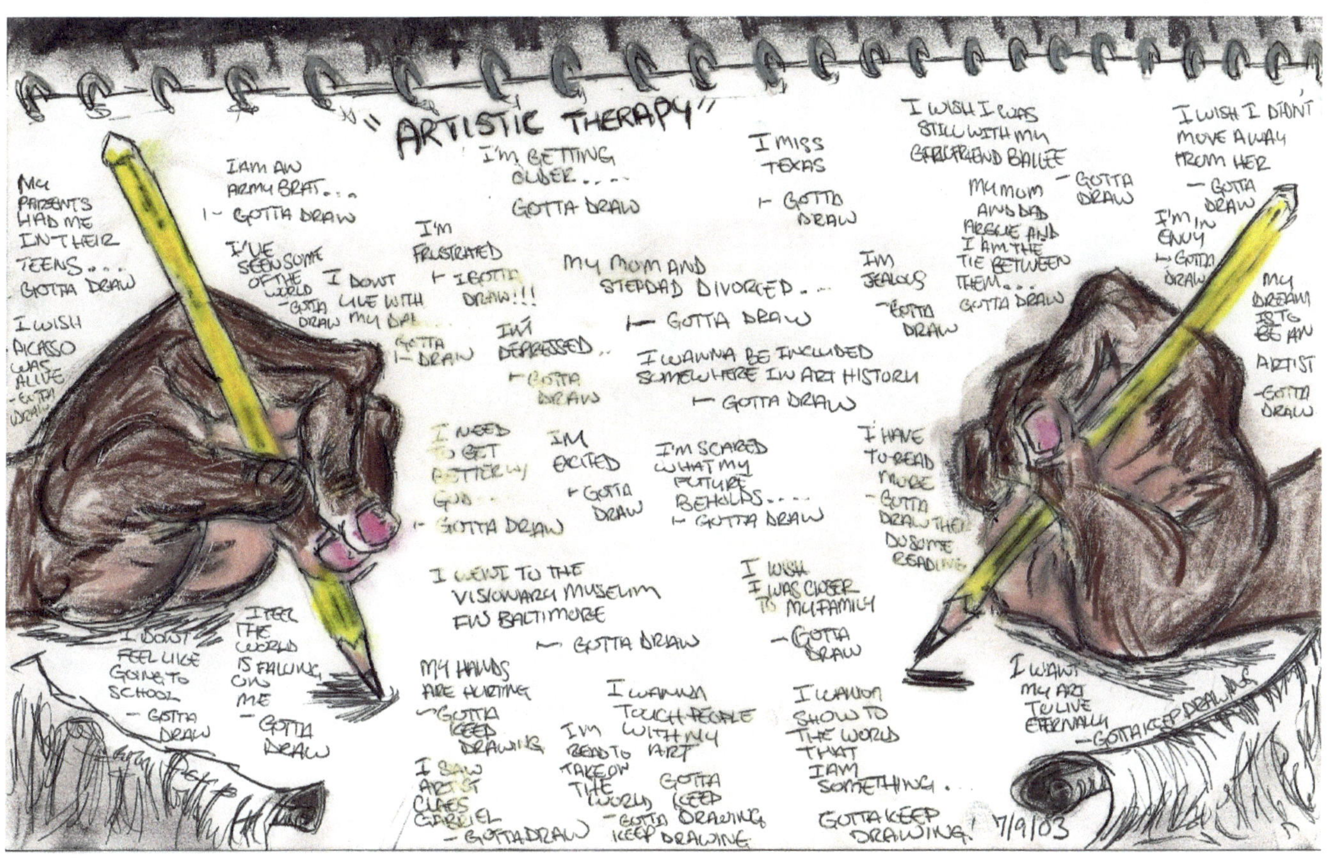

"Artistic Therapy" **(2003)**

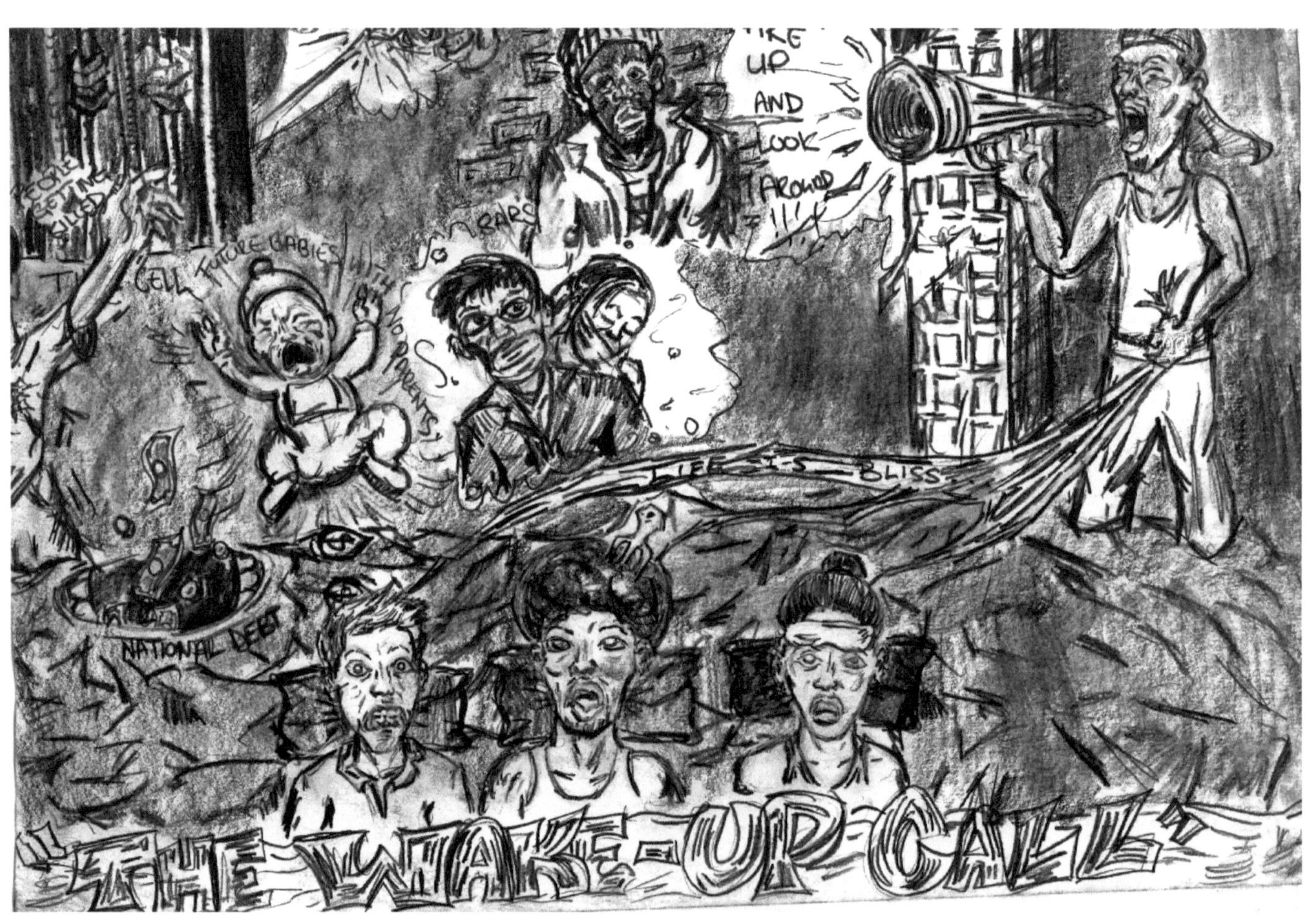

"The Wake-Up call" **(2003)**

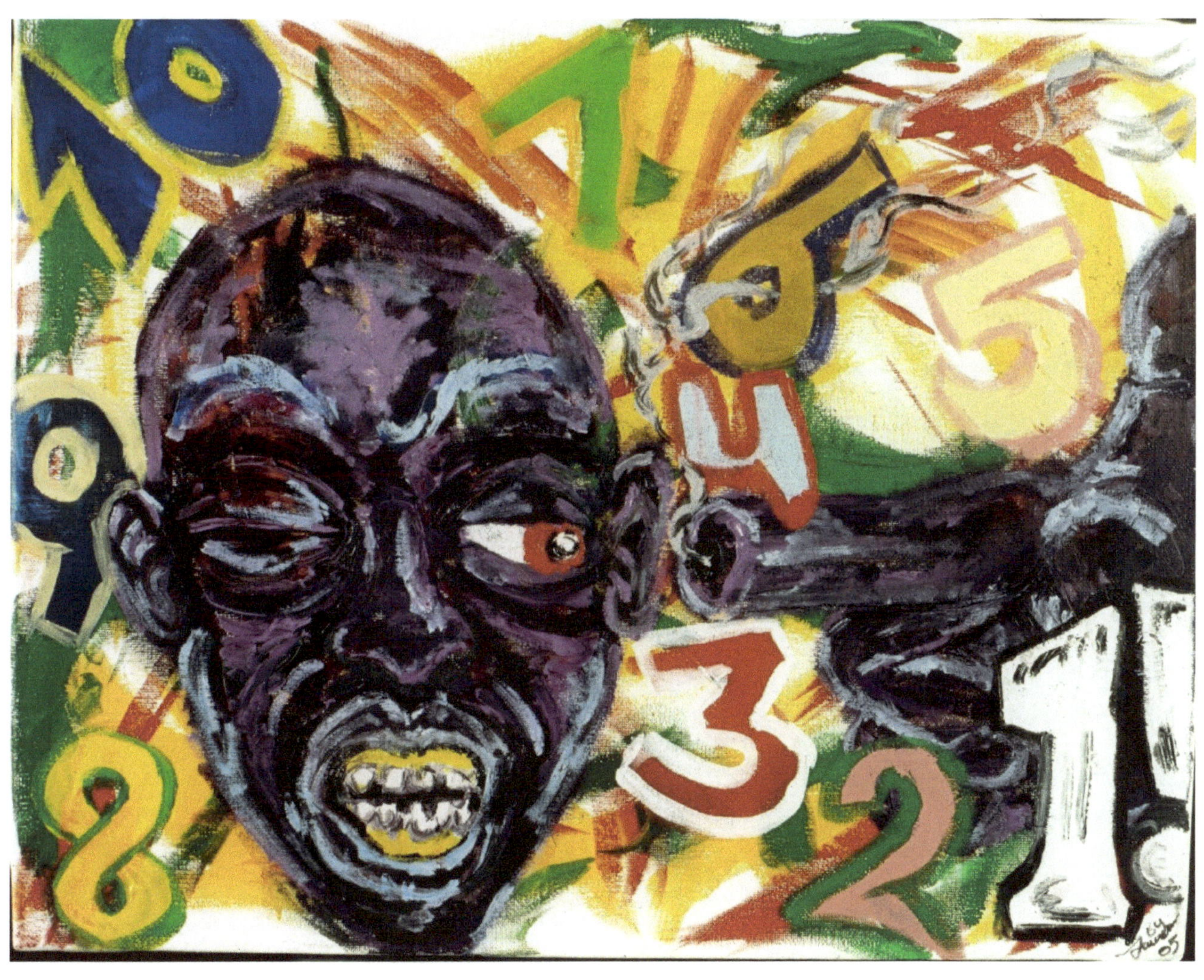

"Countdown to Self-Destruction" **(2004)**

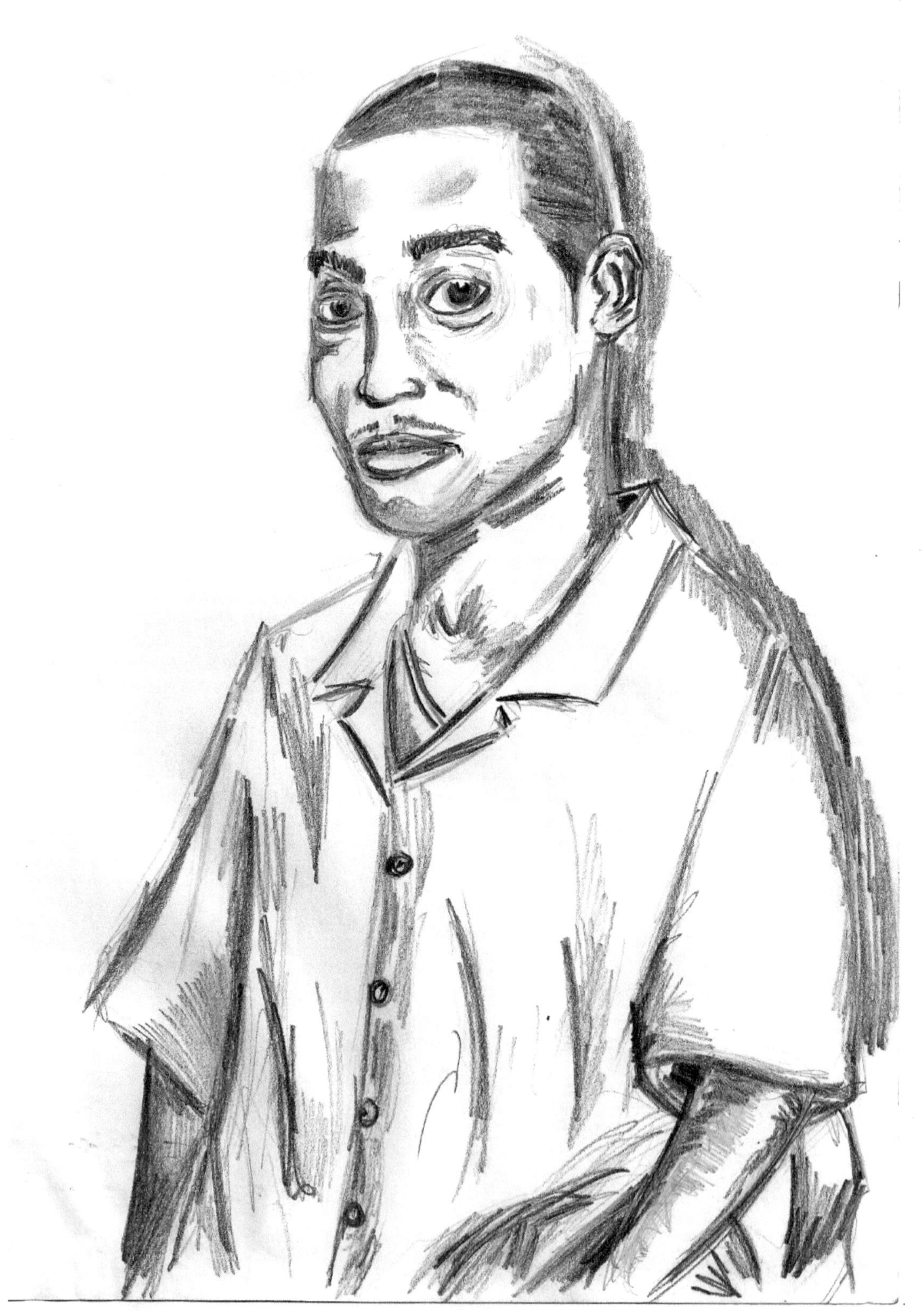

"Self-Portrait at age 18" **(2004)**

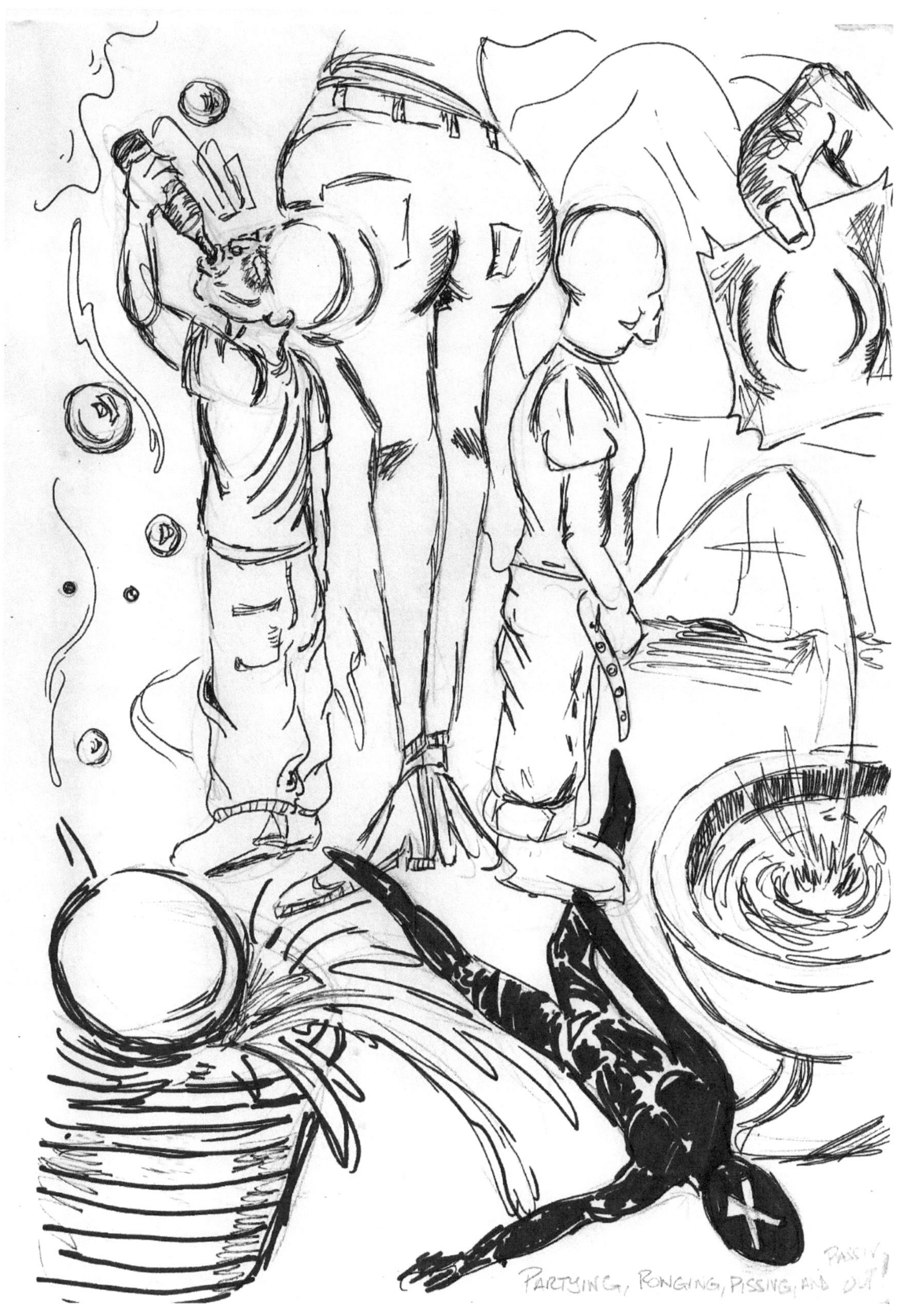

"P4 (Partying, Ponging, Pissing, and Passing Out)" **(2005)**

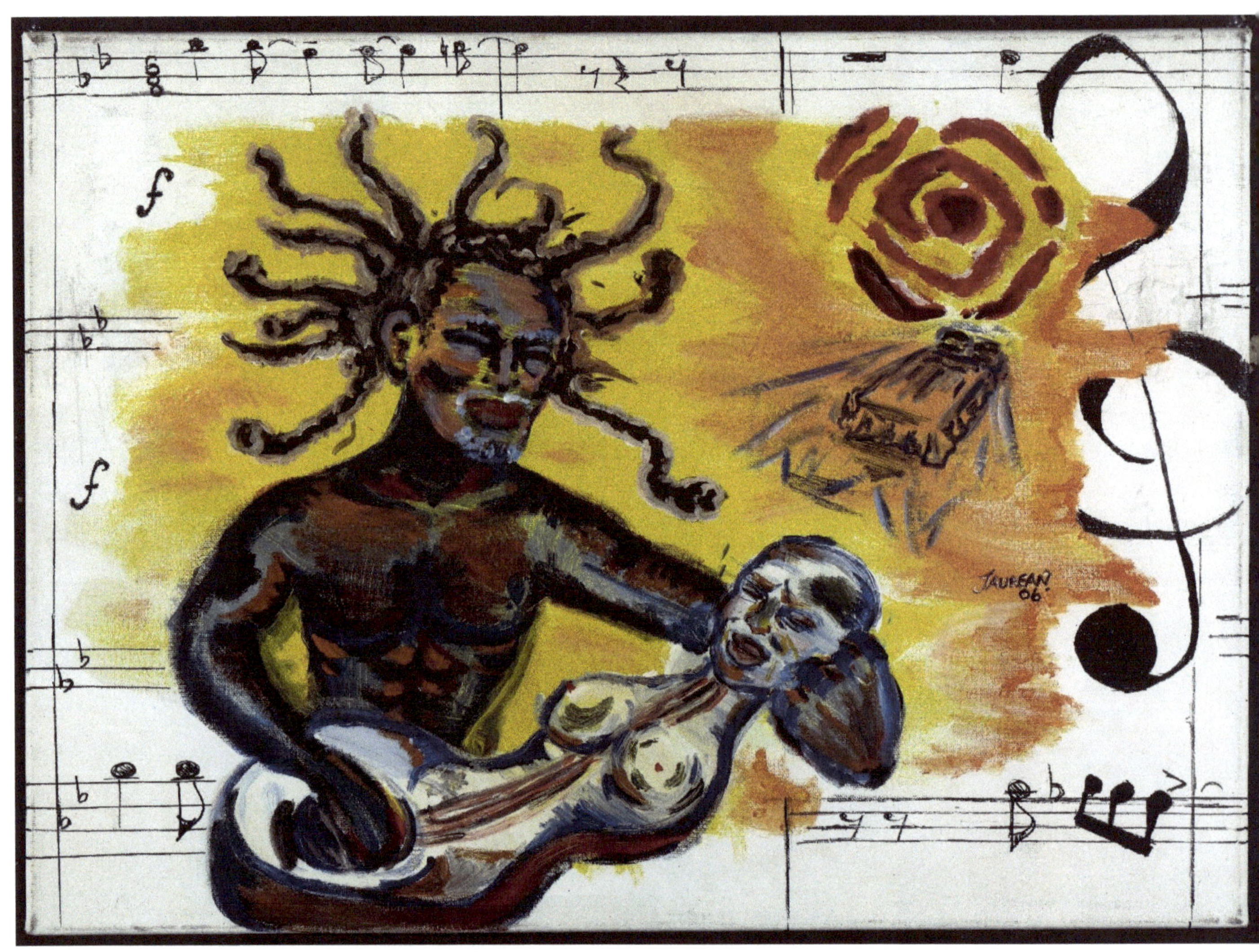

"The Instrumental" **(2006)**

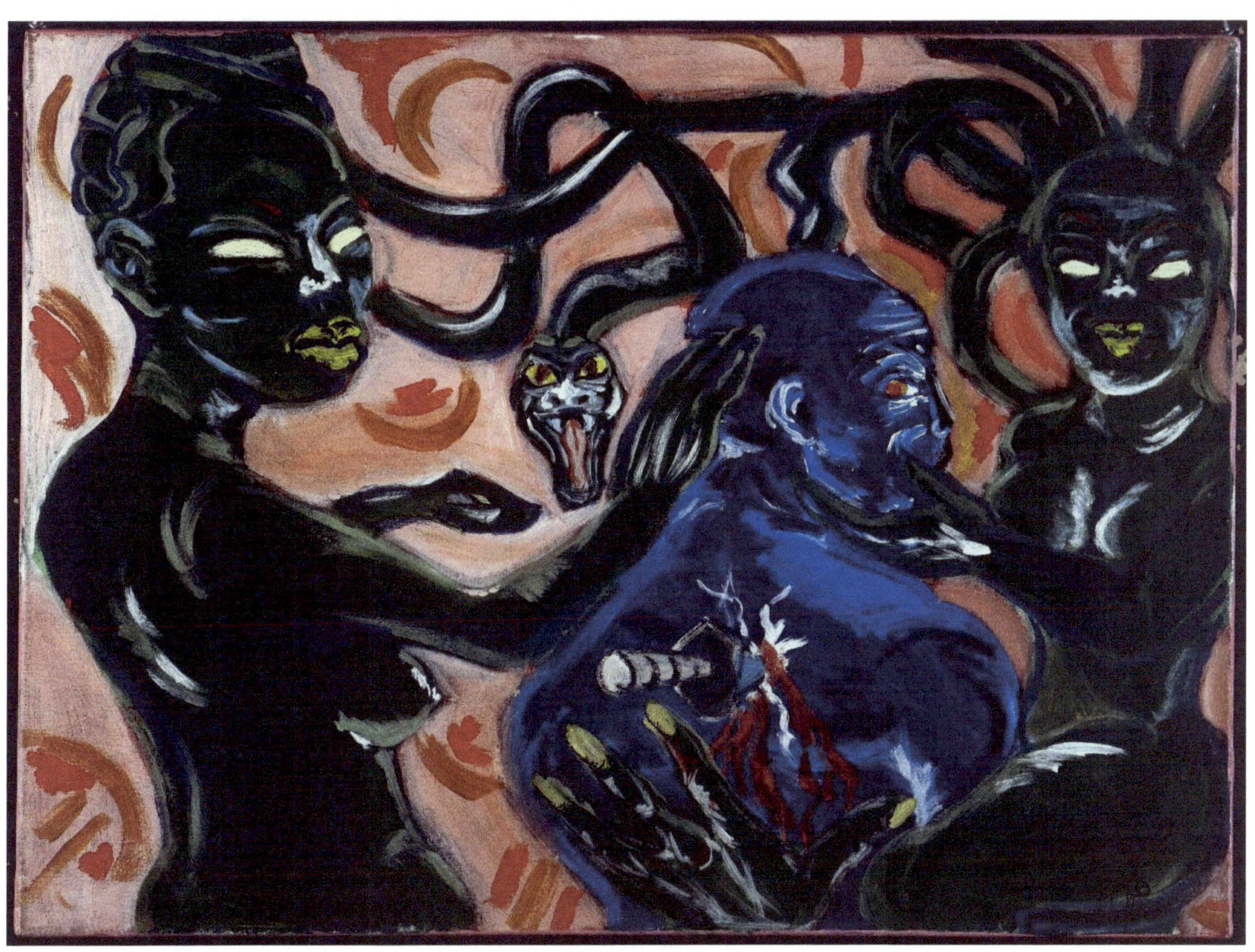

"Snakes" **(2006)**

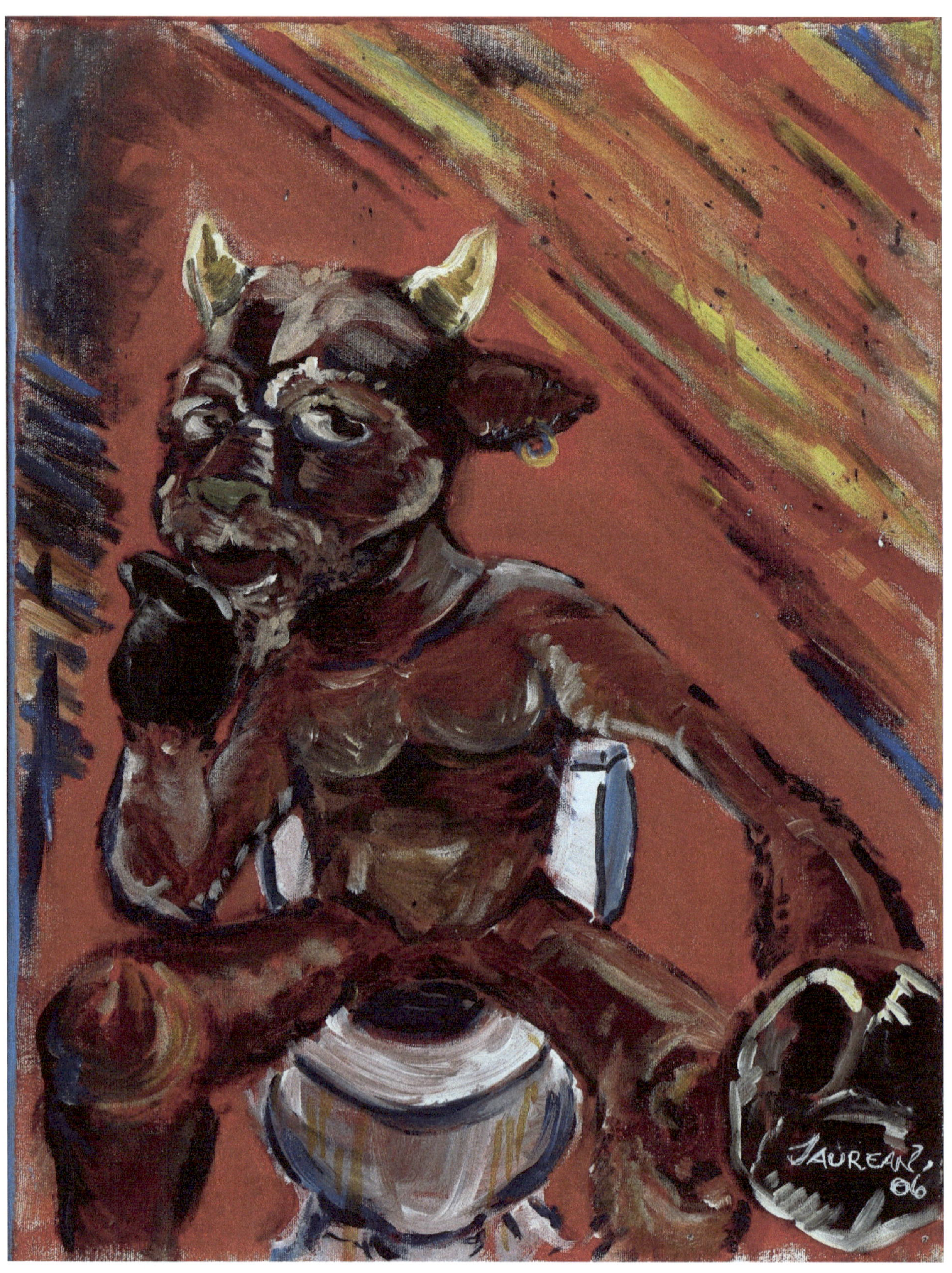

"Bullshit" **(2006)**

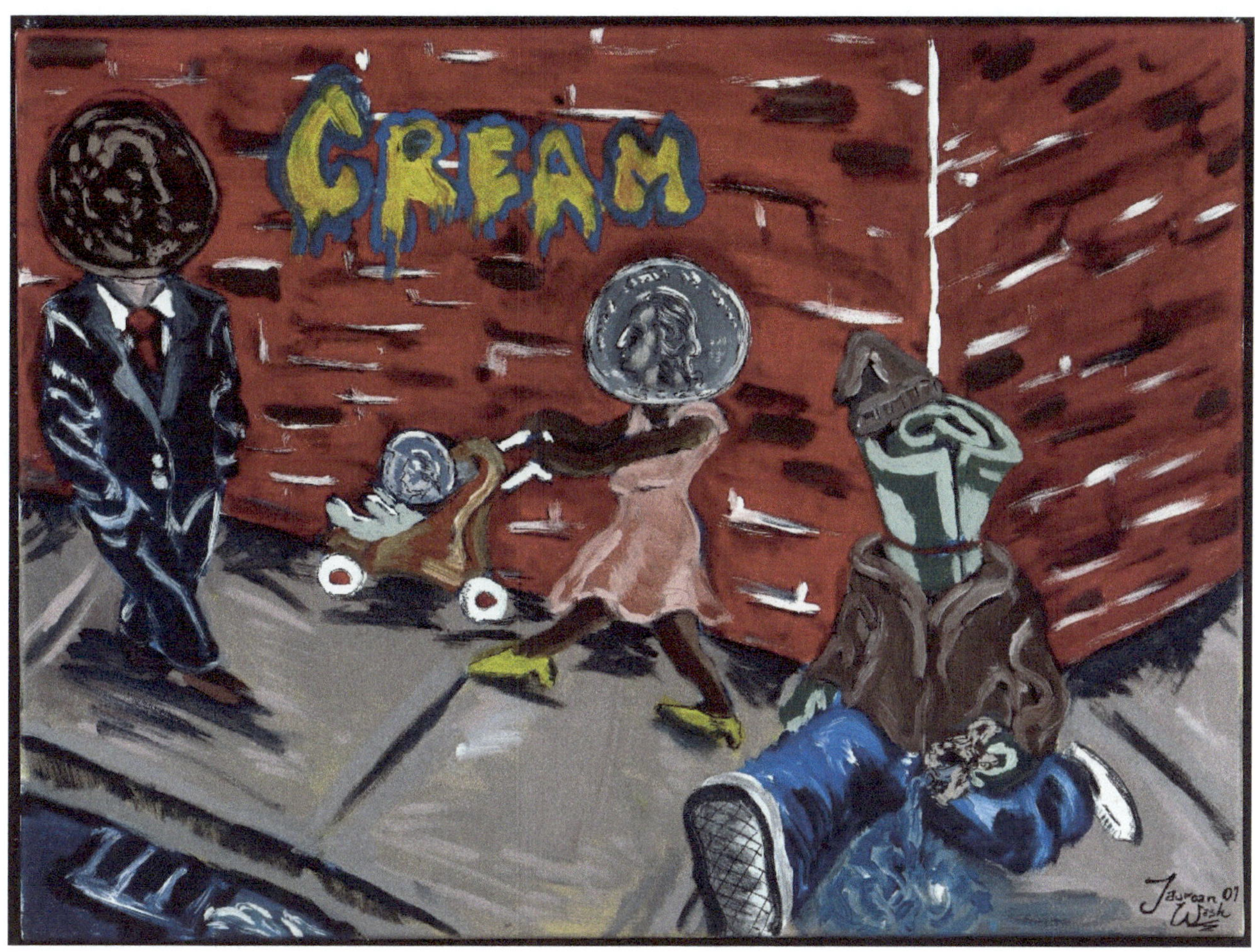

"Self-Worth" **(2007)**

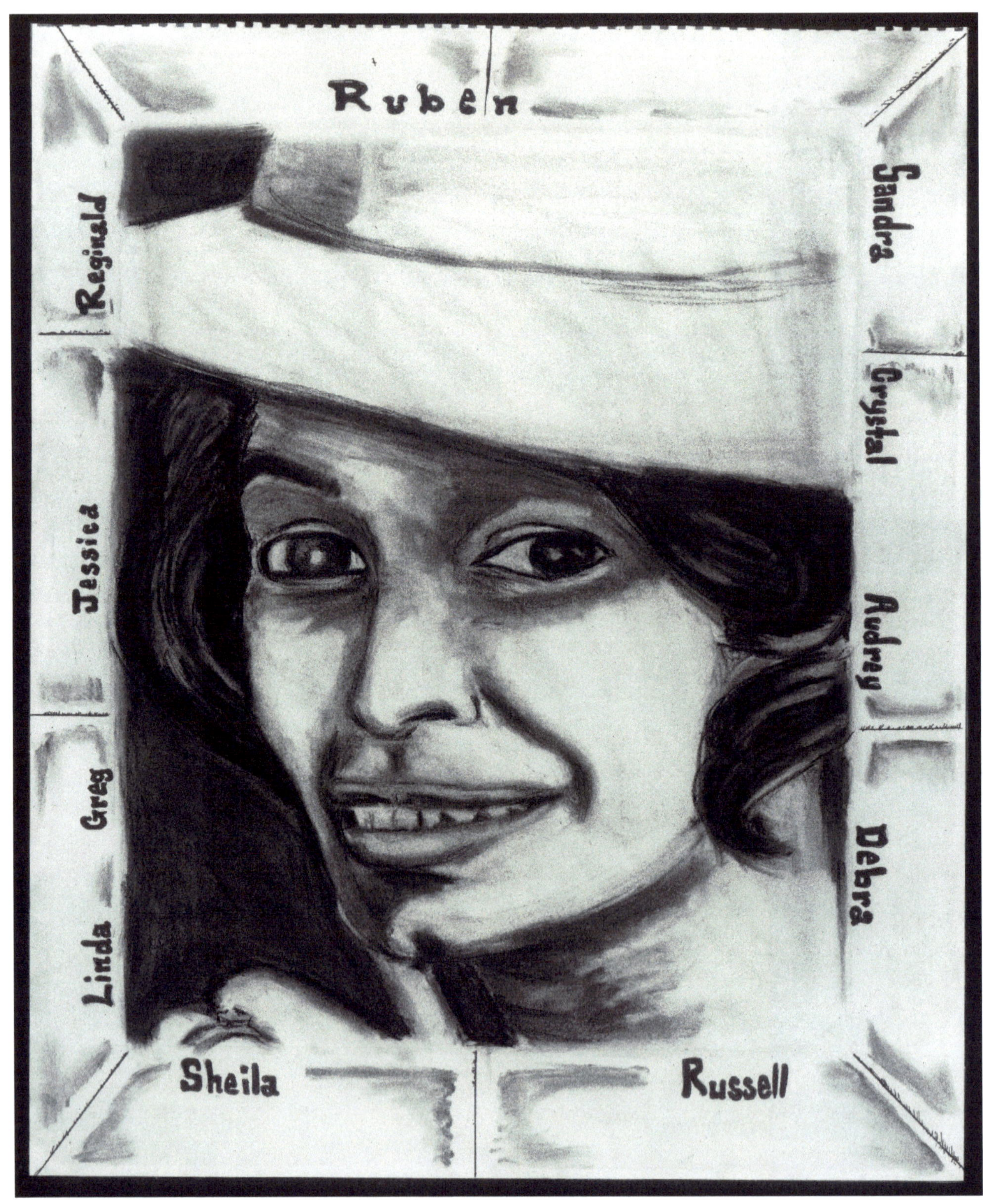

"Vera" **(2008)** *Rest in Peace Granny I love you

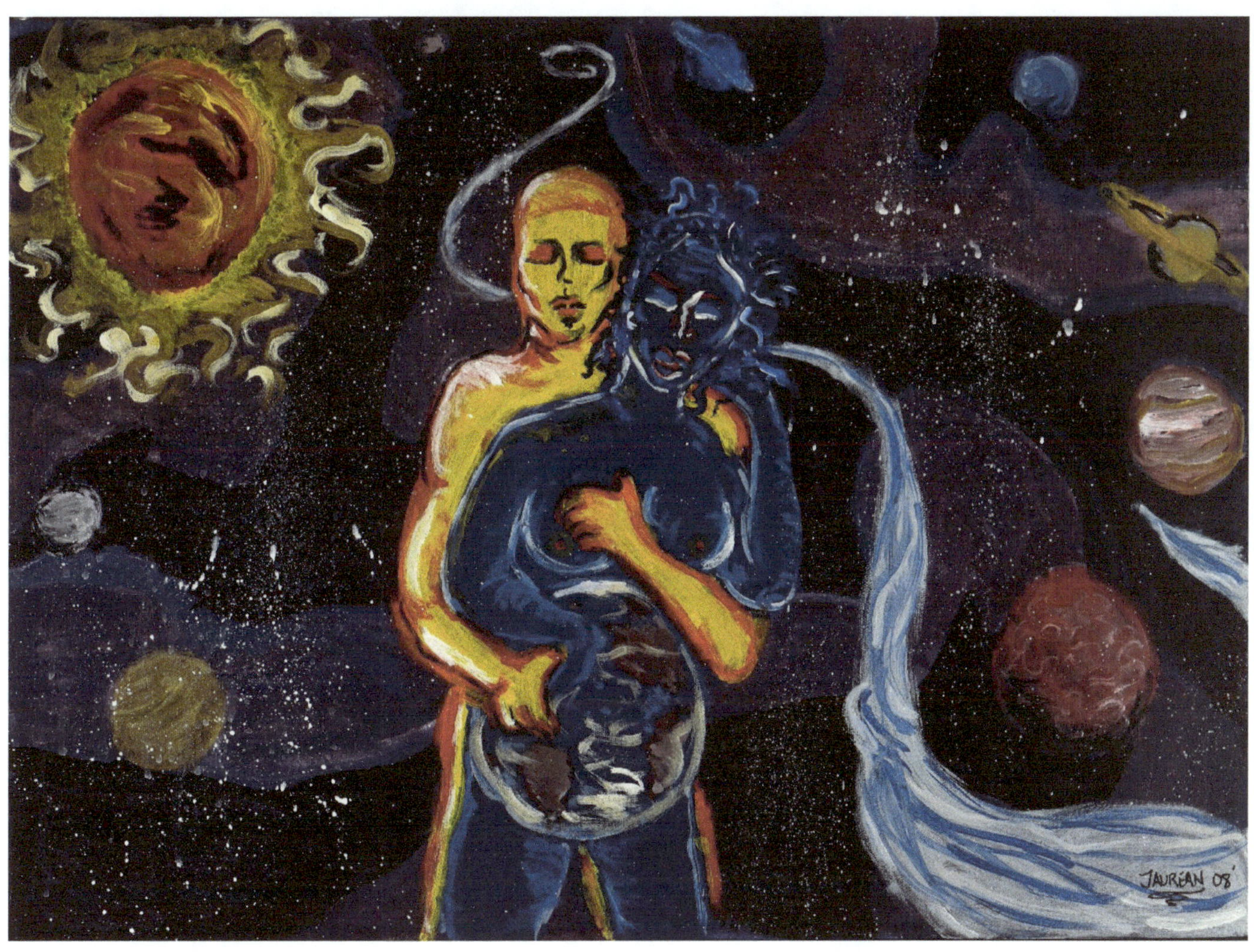

"A New World" **(2008)**

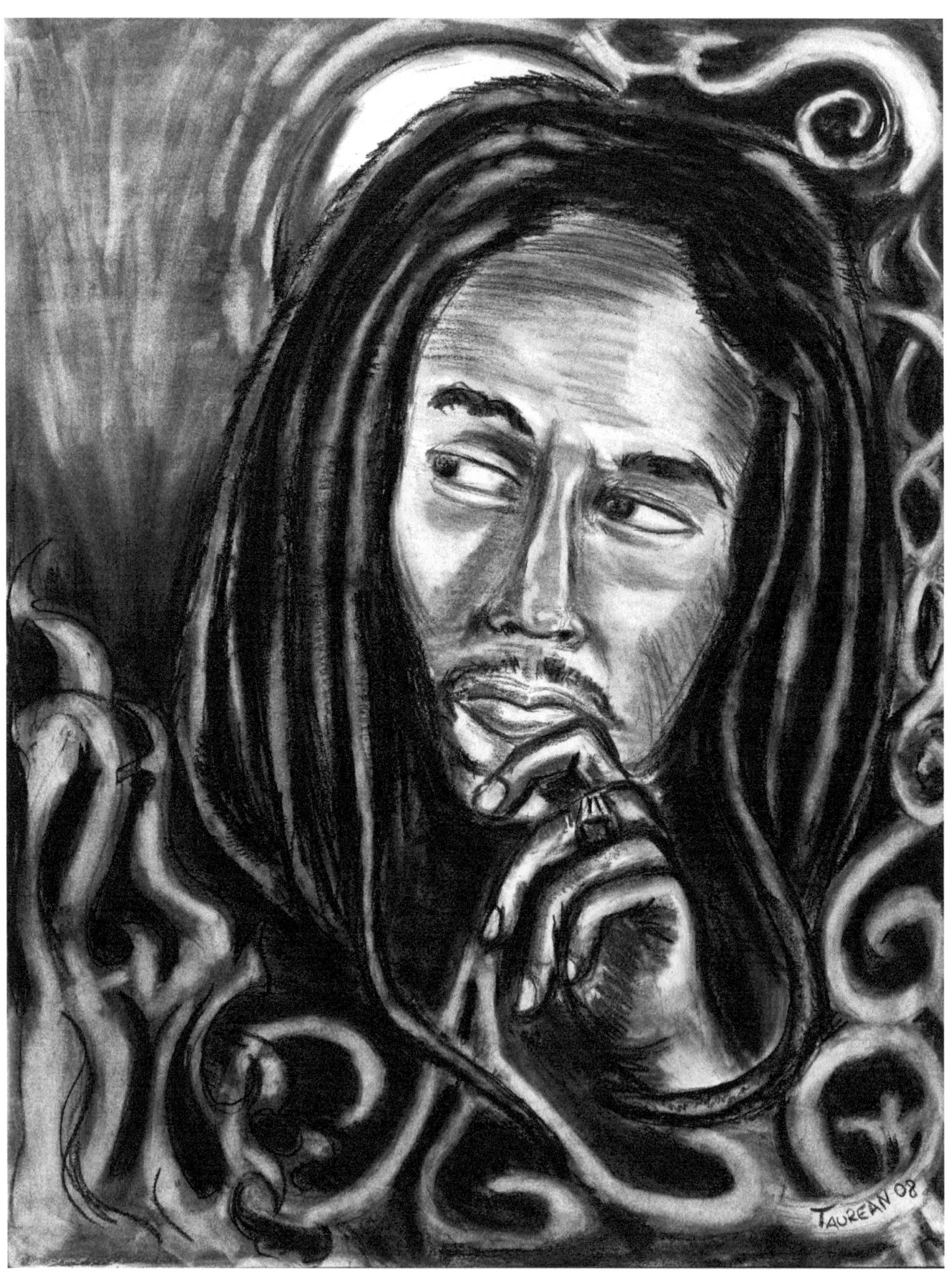

"Bob Marley" **(2008)**

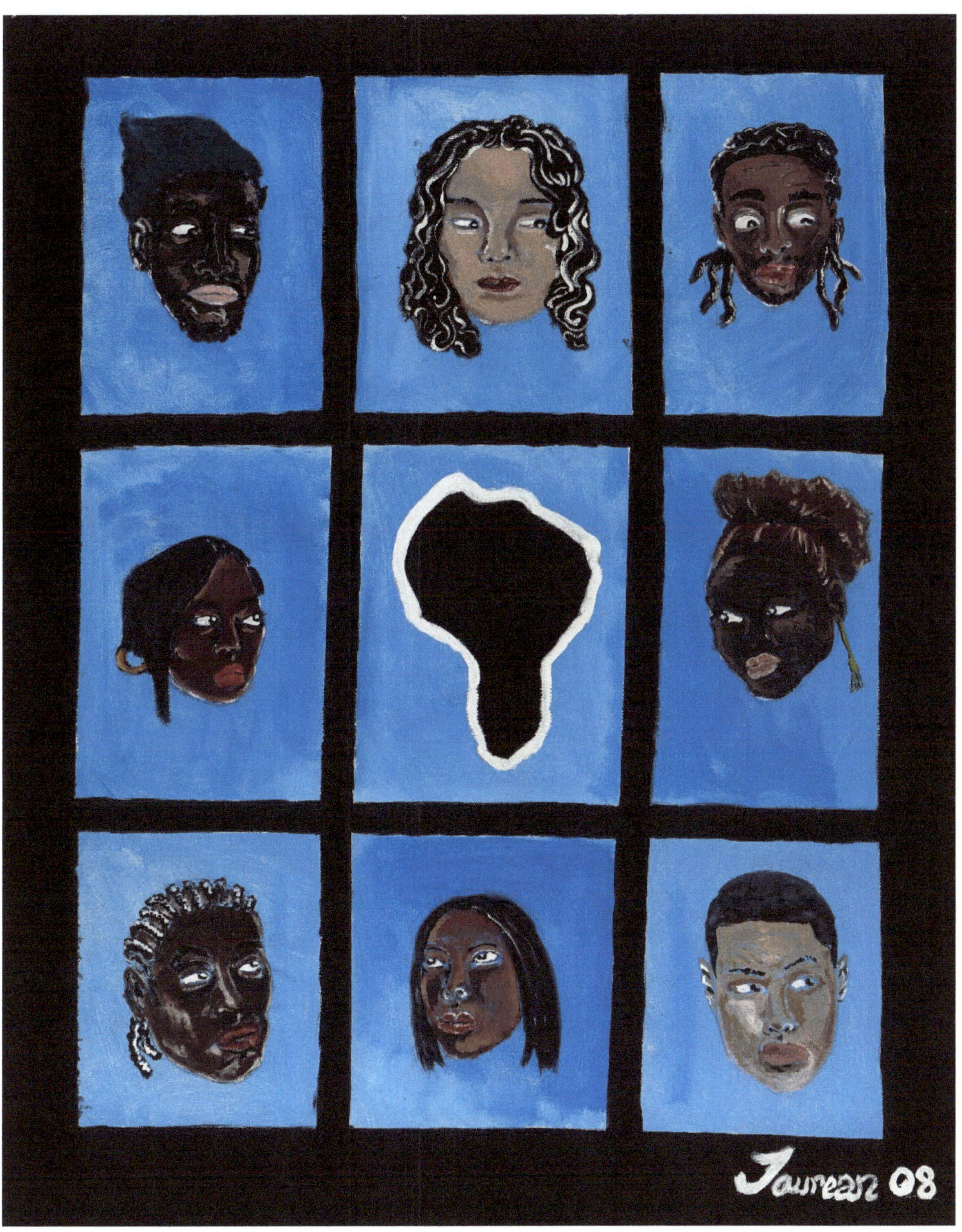

"Color Schemes" **(2008)**

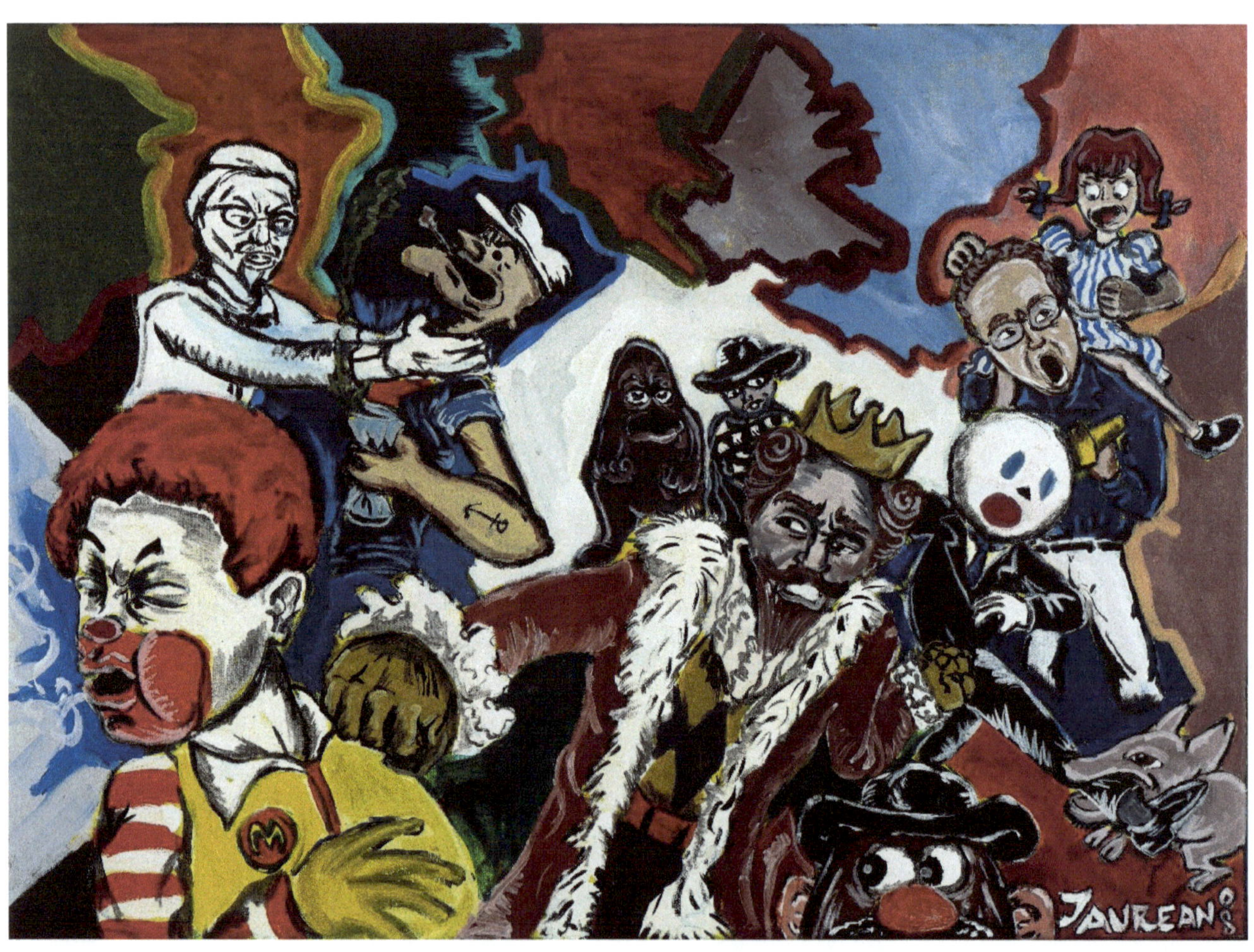

"Fast Food Franchise Fight" **(2008)**

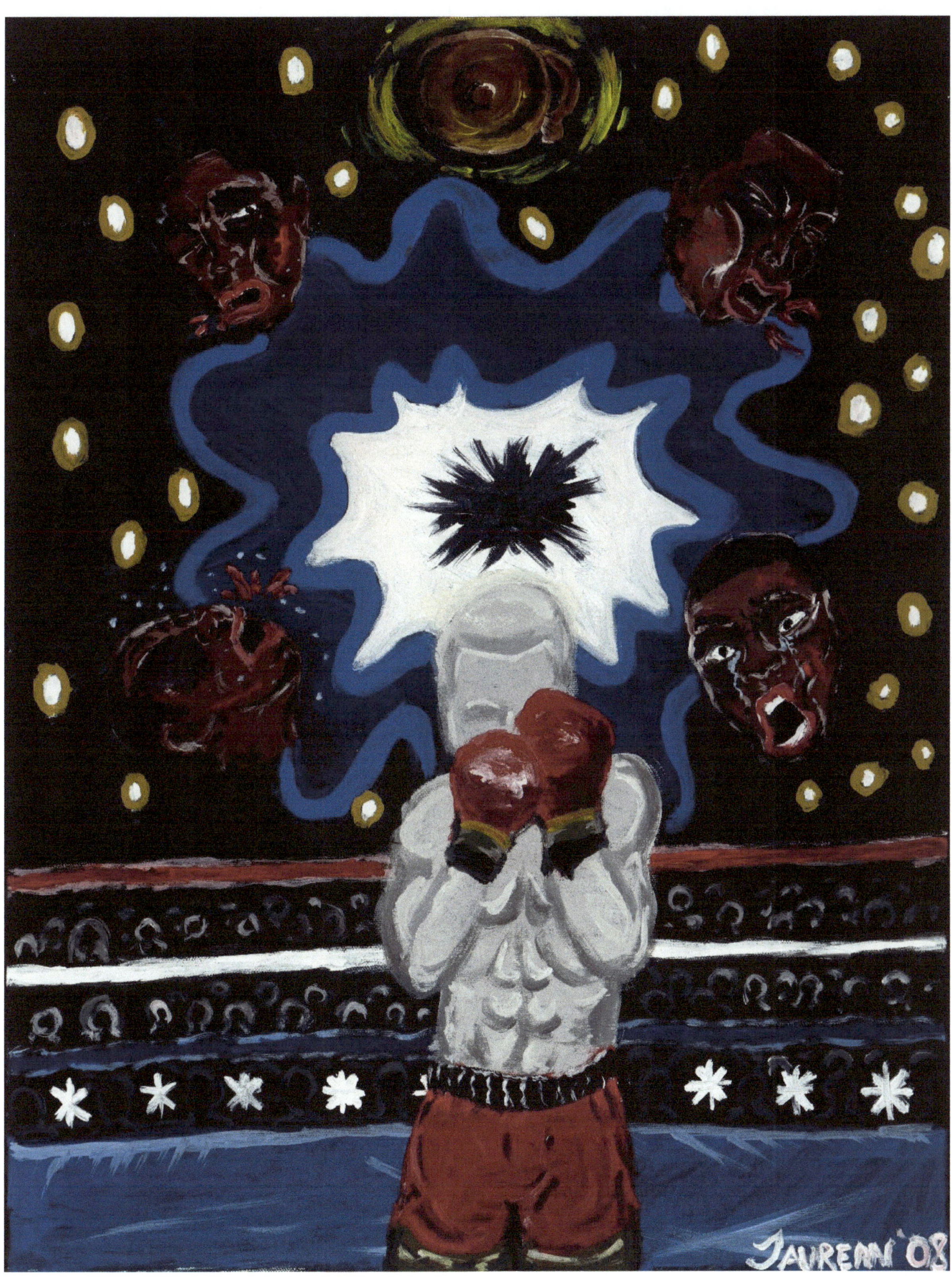

"Rope-A-Dope" **(2008)**

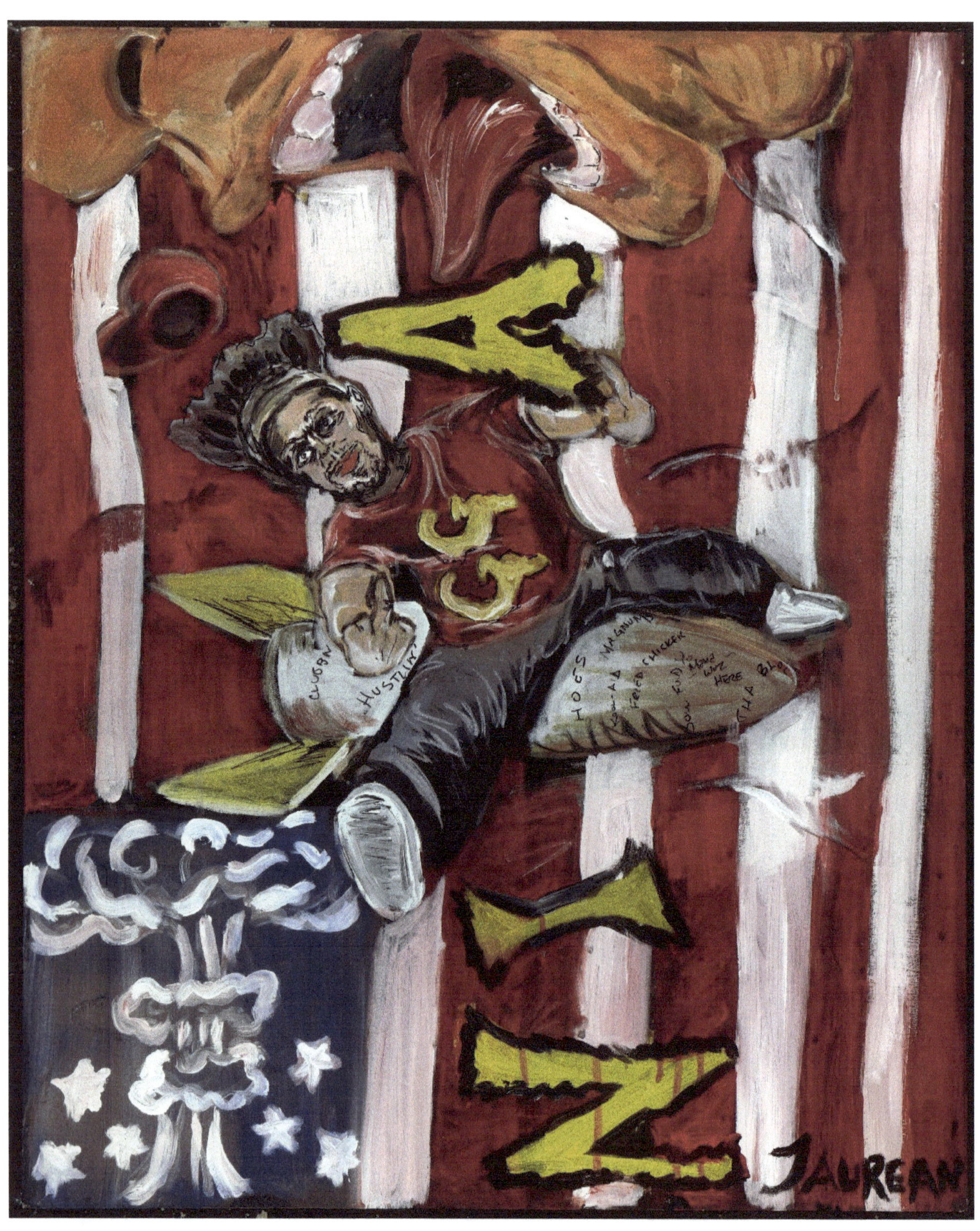

"N-Bomb" **(2008)**

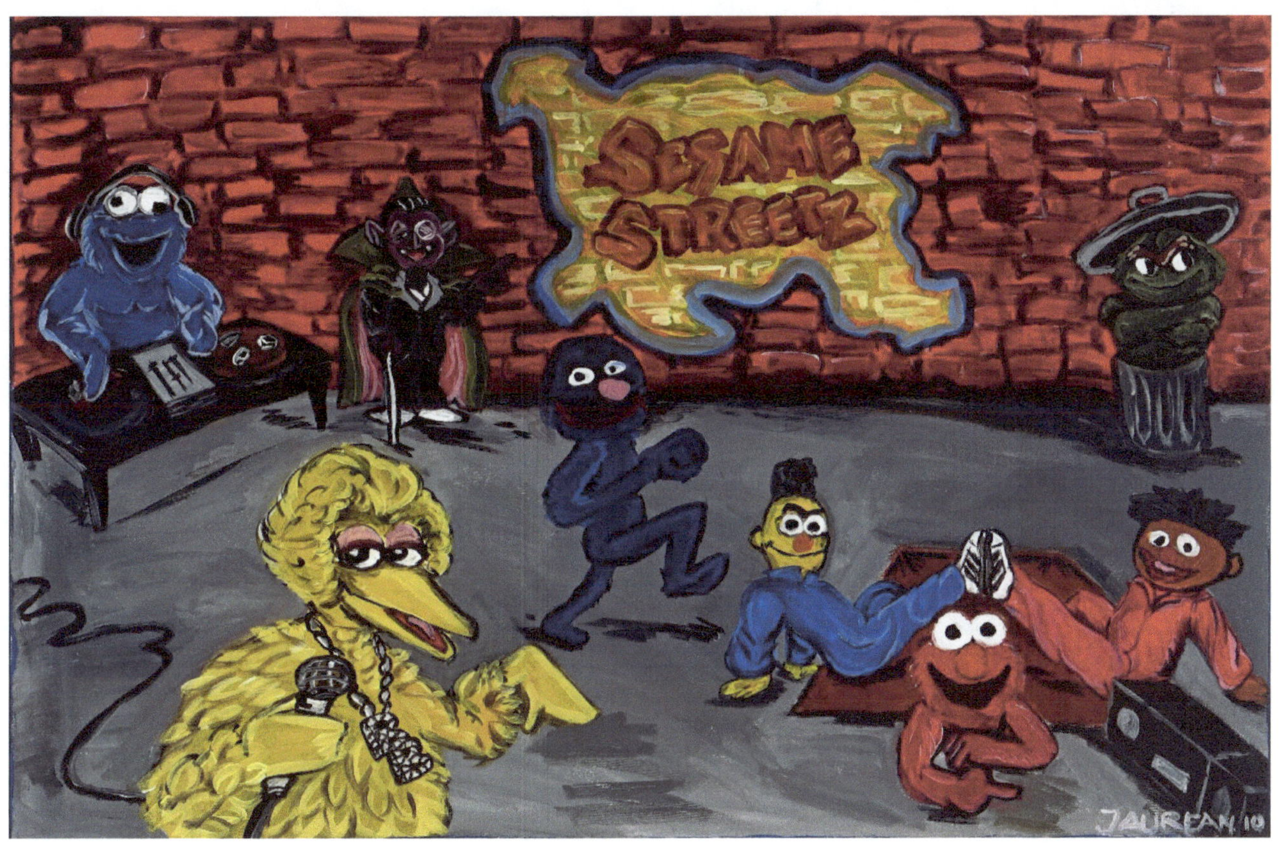

"Sesame Streets" **(2010)**

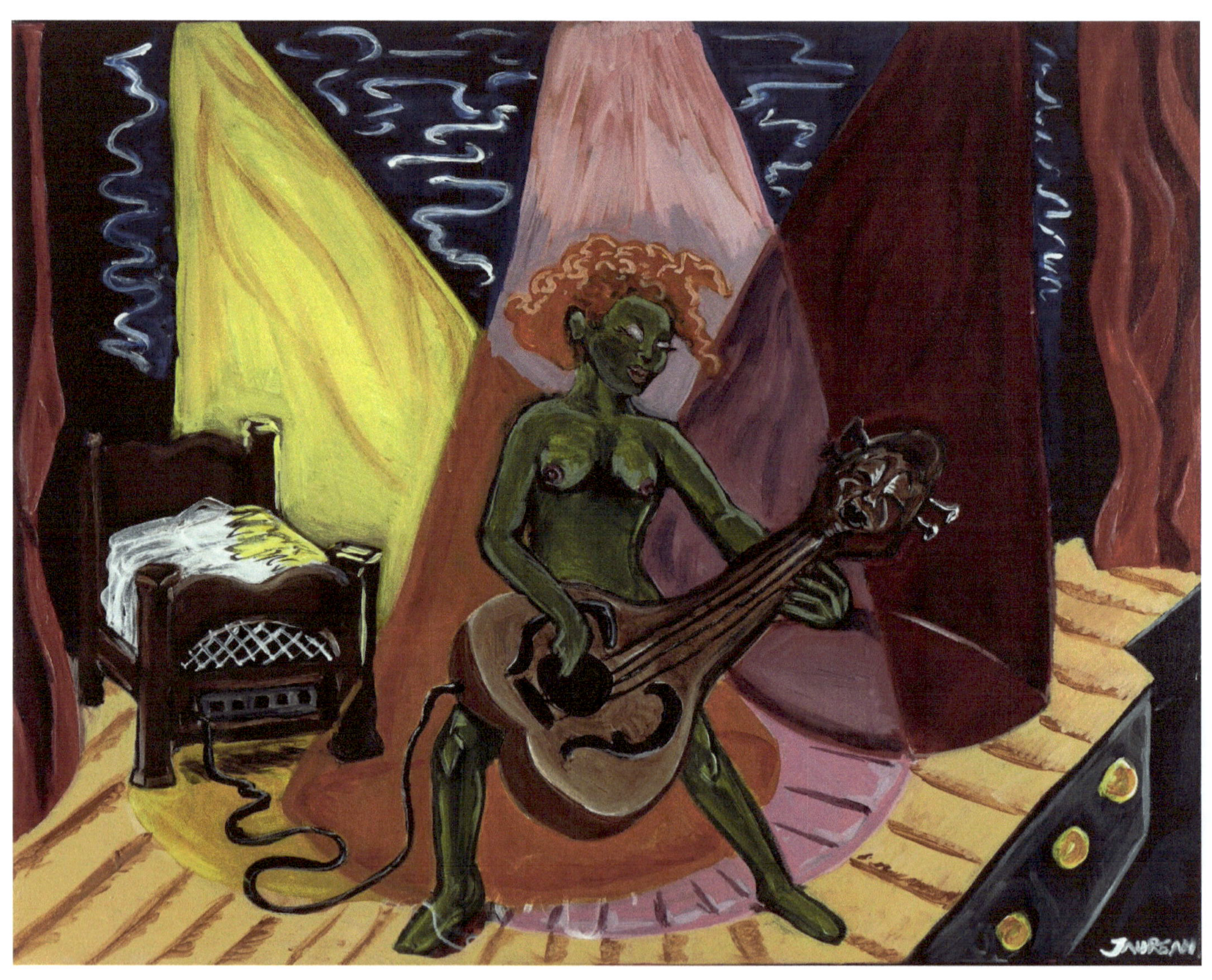

"The Instrumental 2" **(2010)**

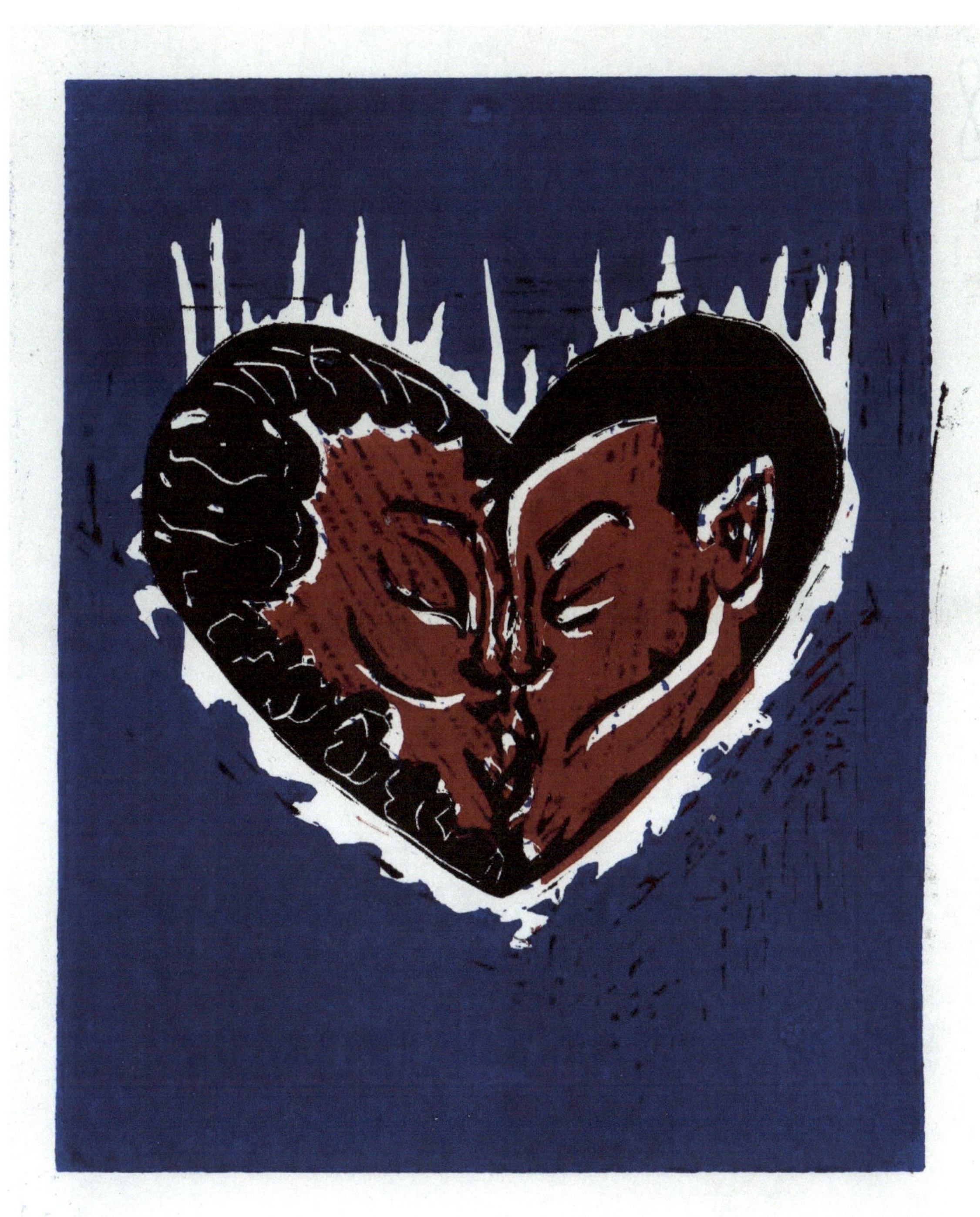

"Lover's Delight" **(2010)** *Big thank you to Andrea McCluskey. You are the best!

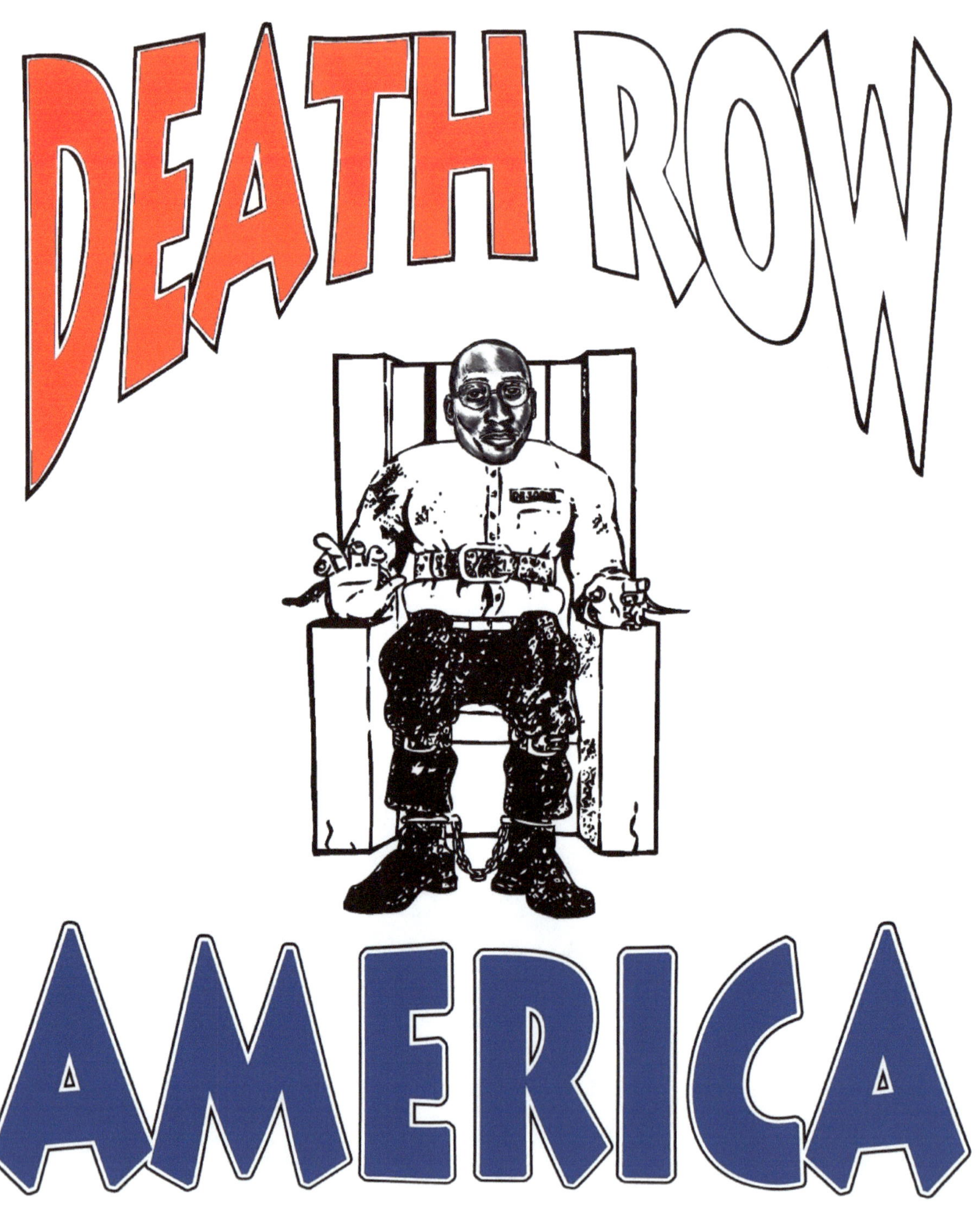

"Troy Davis" **(2011)**

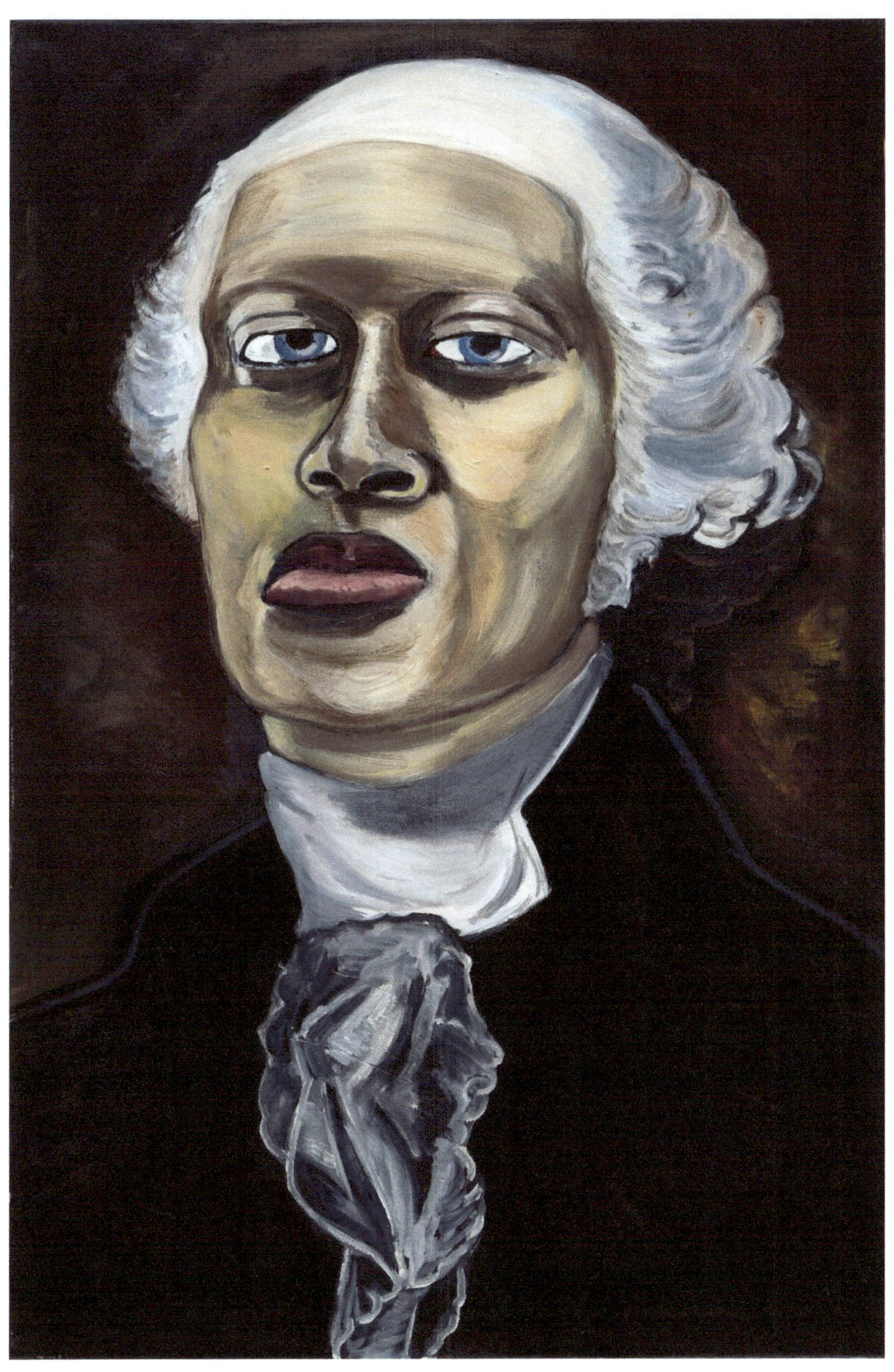

"I AM GEORGE WASHINGTON (Self-Portrait)" **(2011)**

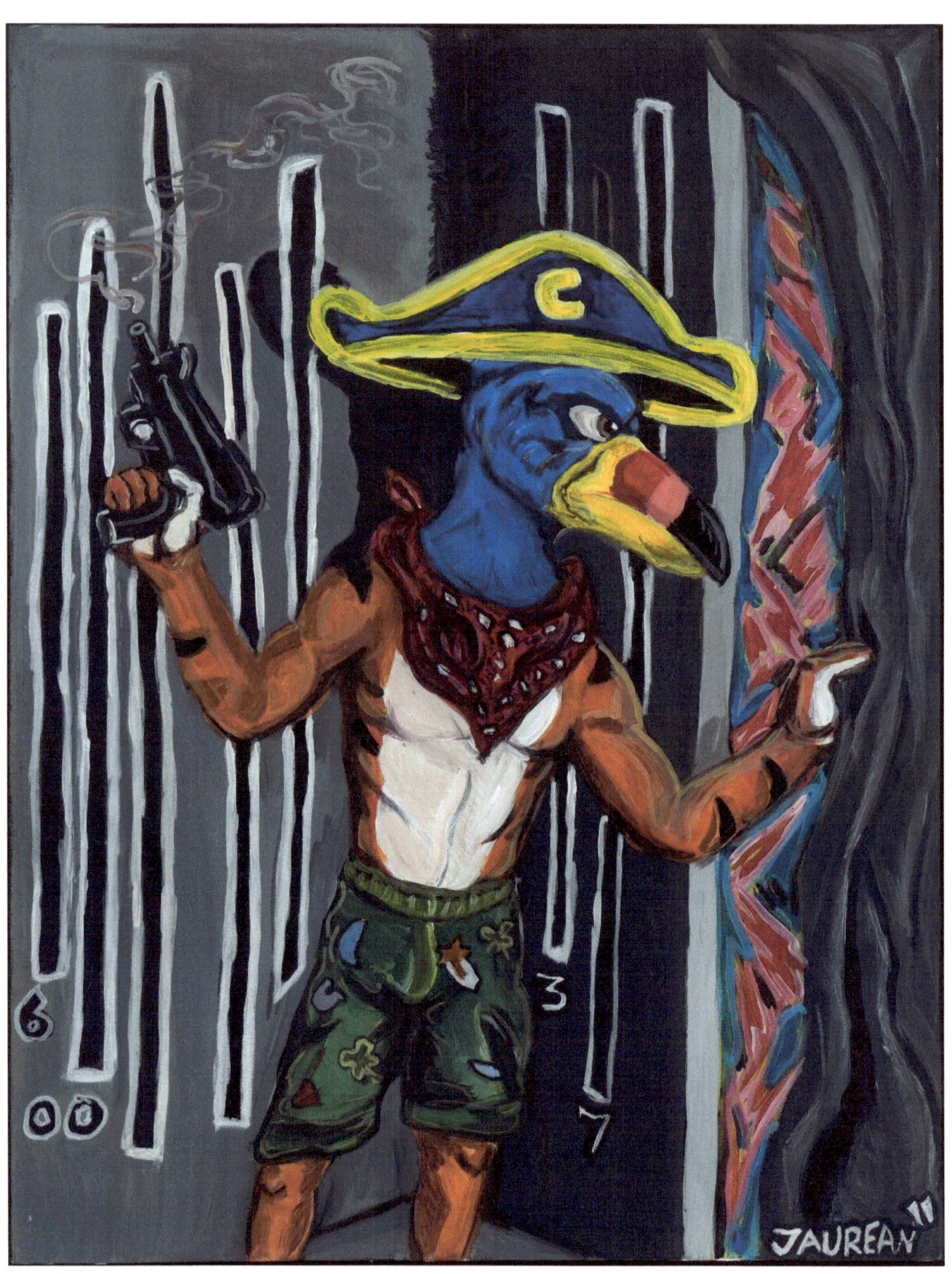

"Cereal Killer" **(2011)**

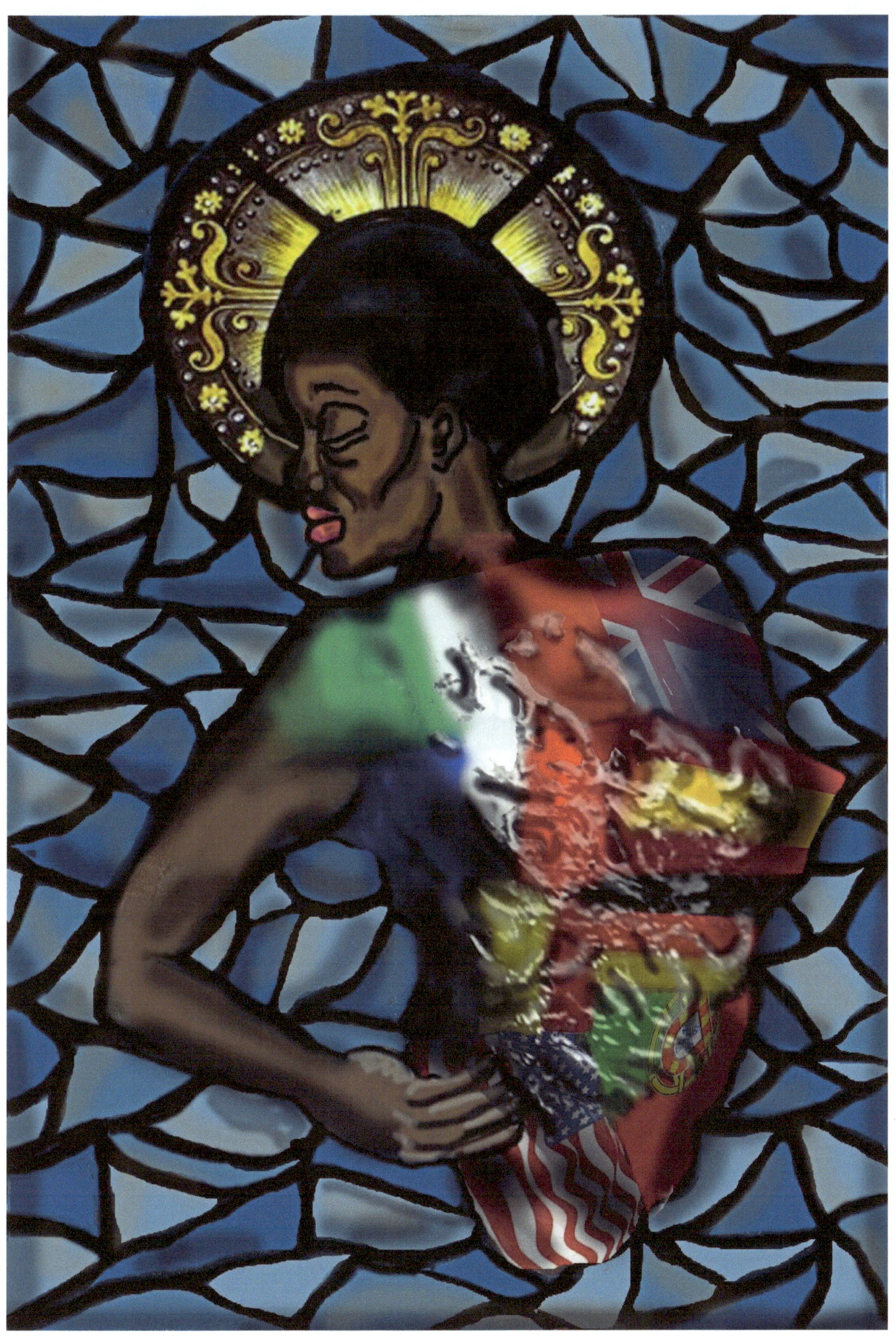

"Afro-Mosaic" **(2011)** *Dr. Tamelyn-Tucker Worgs inspired this piece with her college class

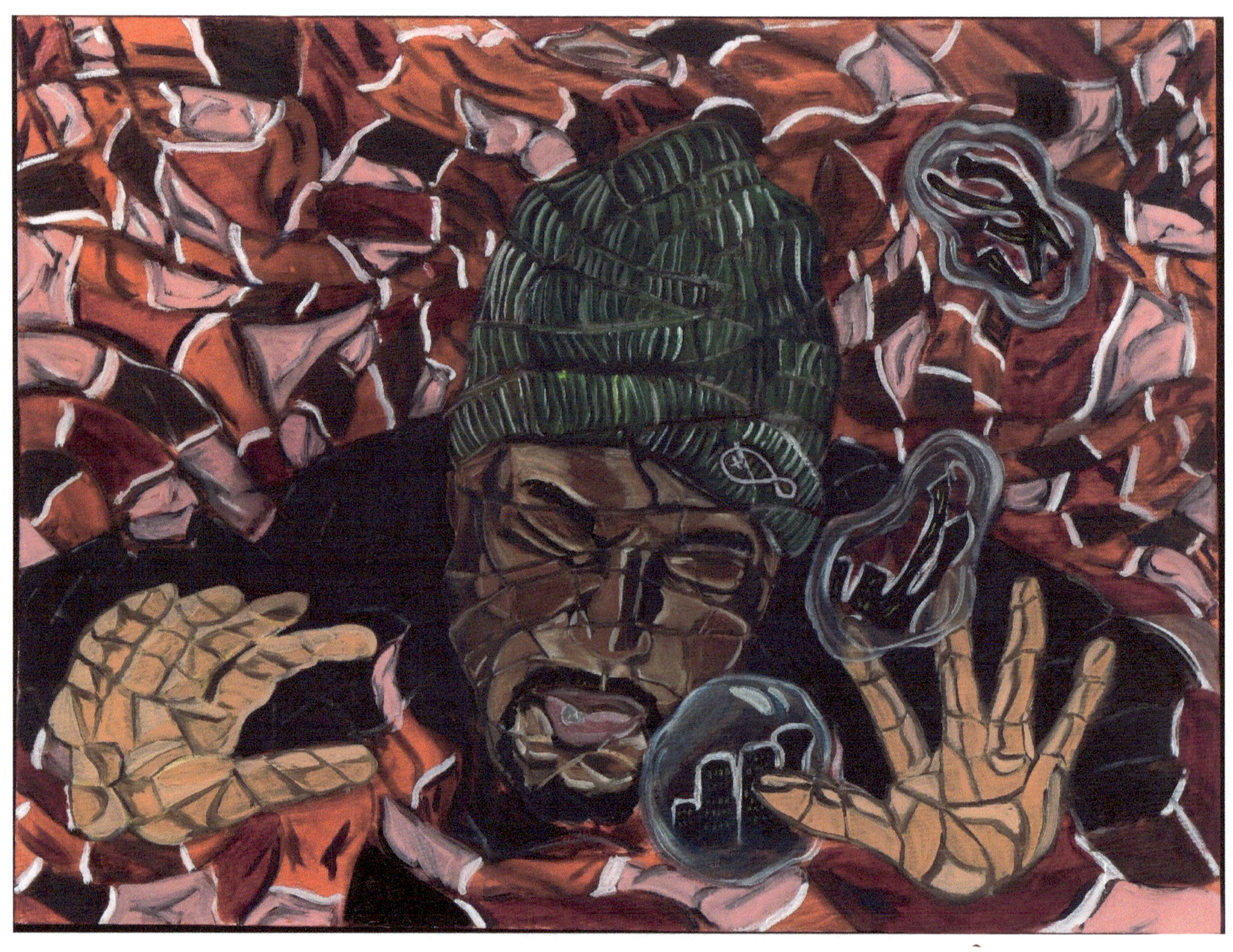

"Drowning Above Water" (Self-Portrait) **(2011)** *Thank you Dr. Ross for believing in me

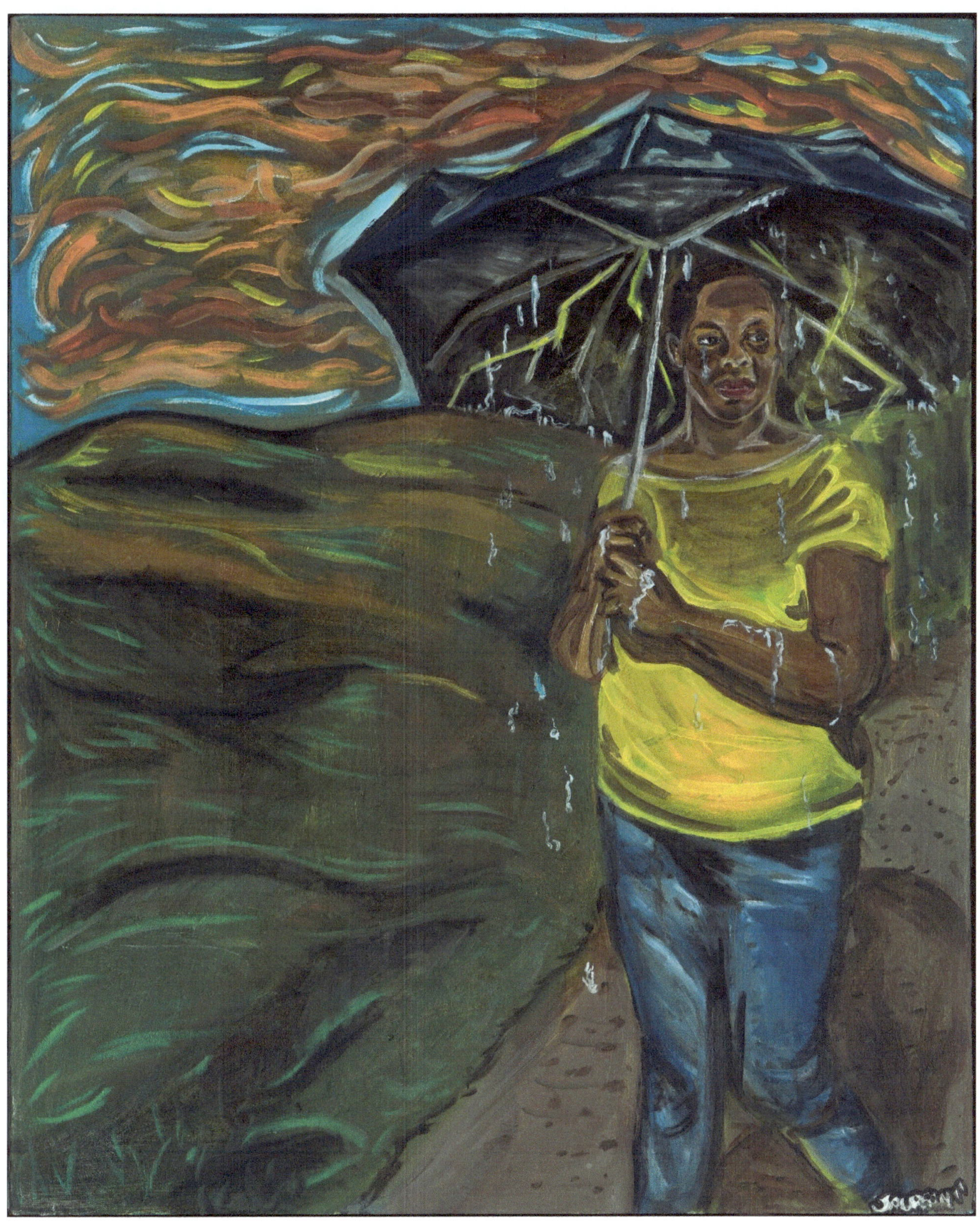

"In The Rain" **(2011)**

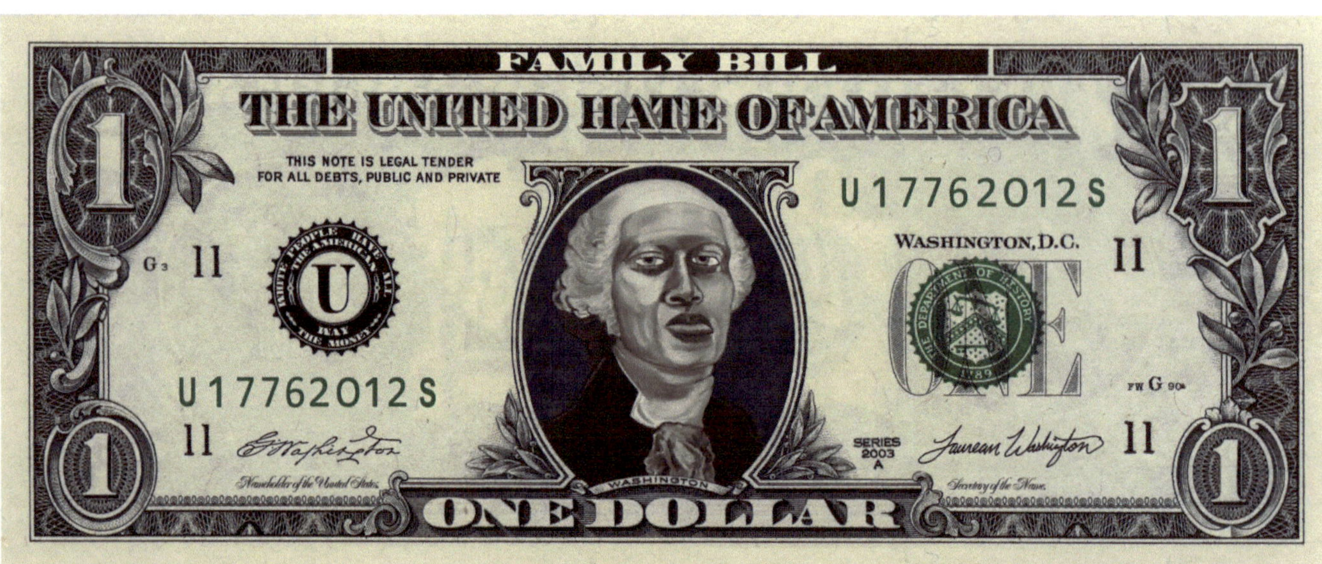

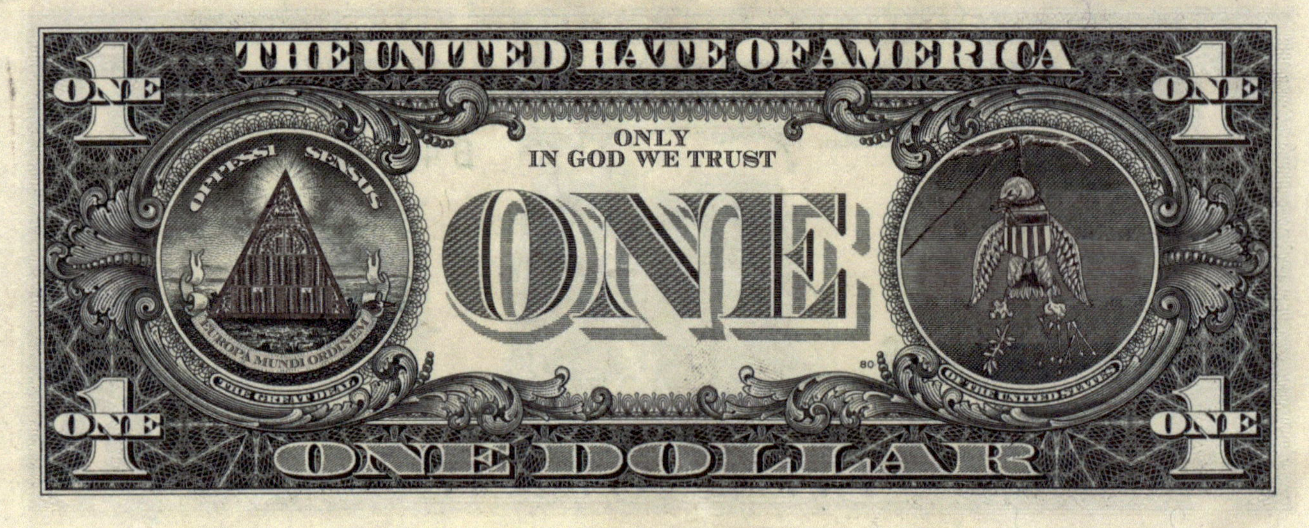

"Family Bill" **(2012)**

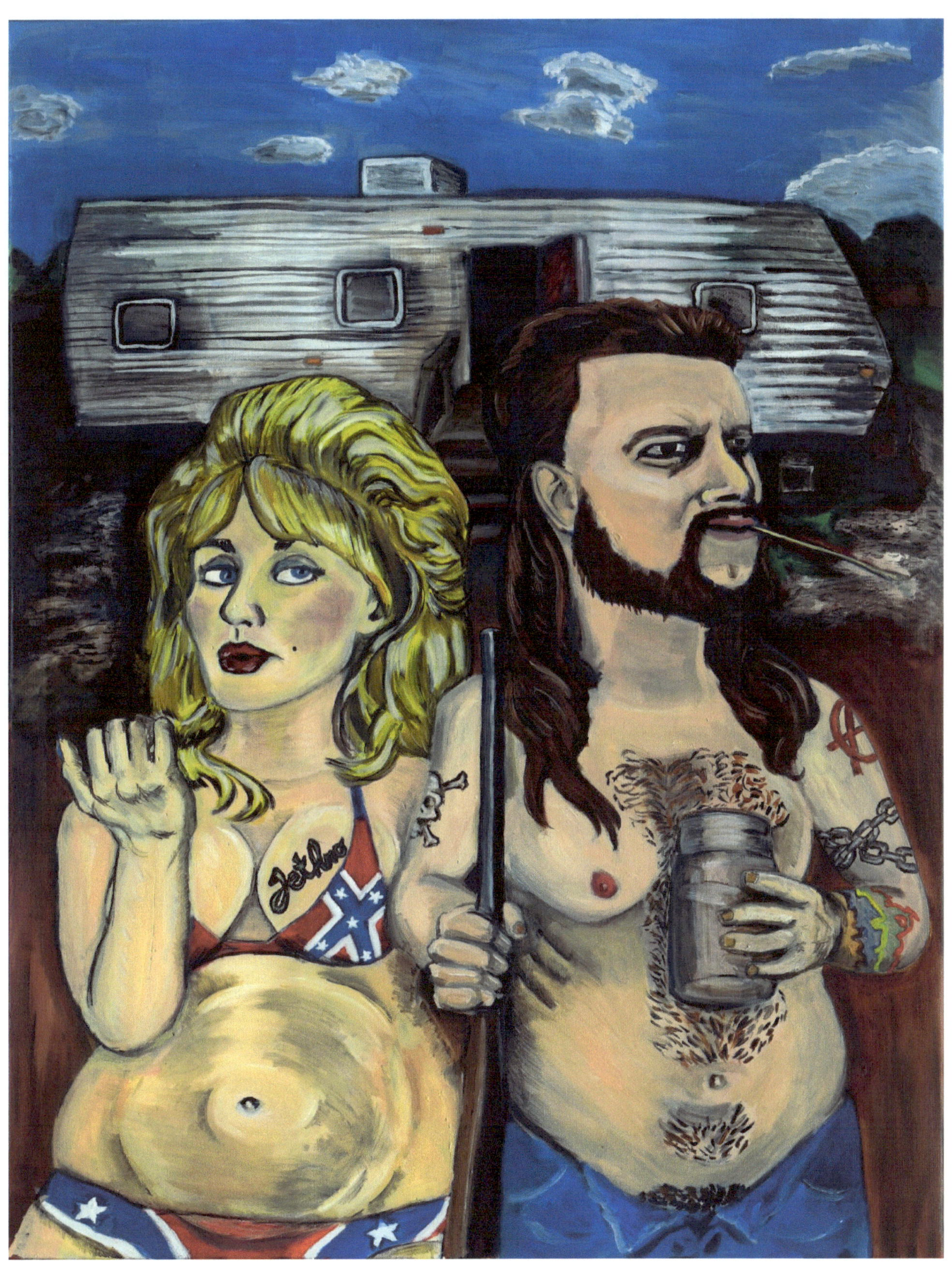

"Rednecks (American Gothic Remix)" **(2013)**

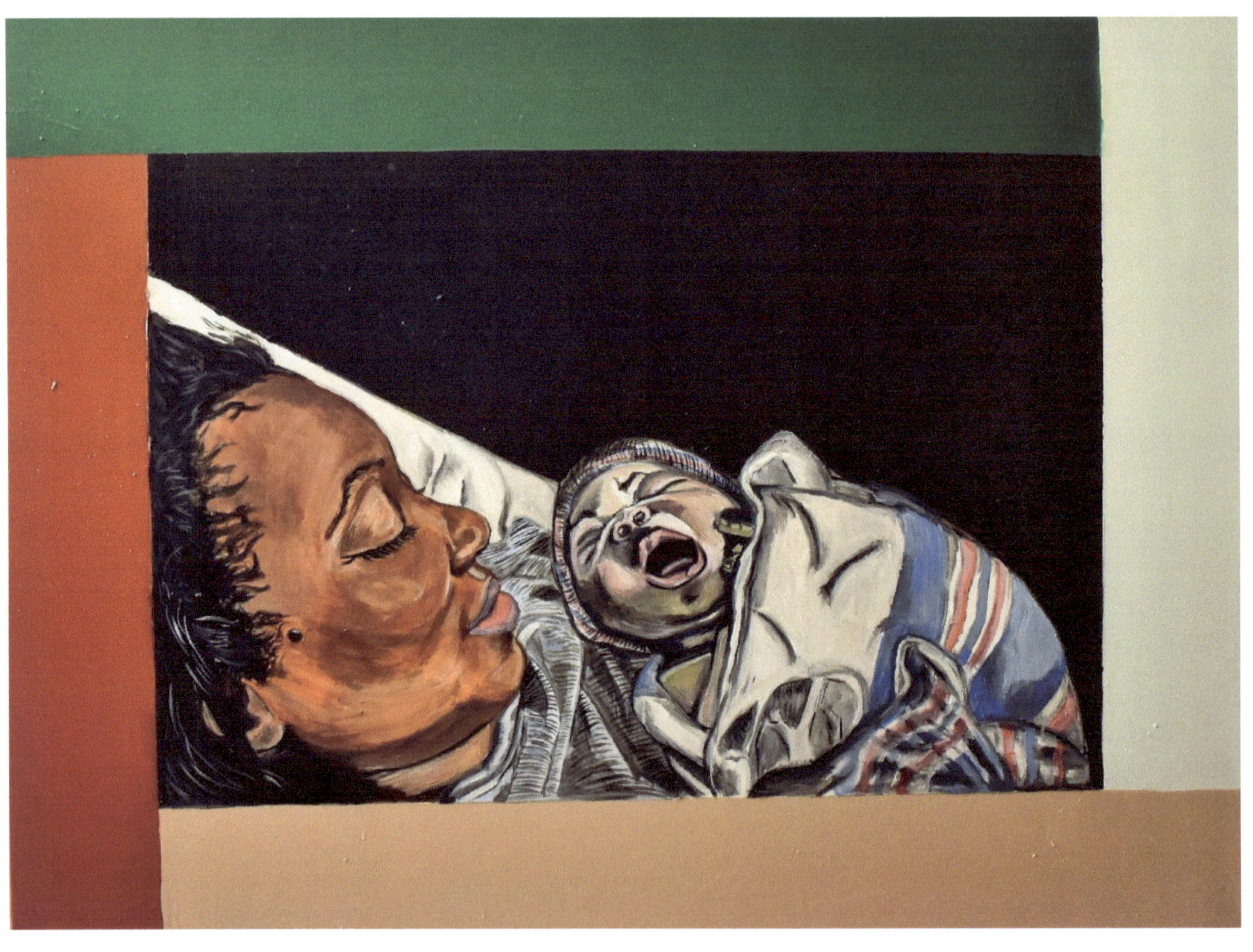

"Pride and Joy" **(2013)** *Blessed by my wife to bring our first born into this world. Love you both

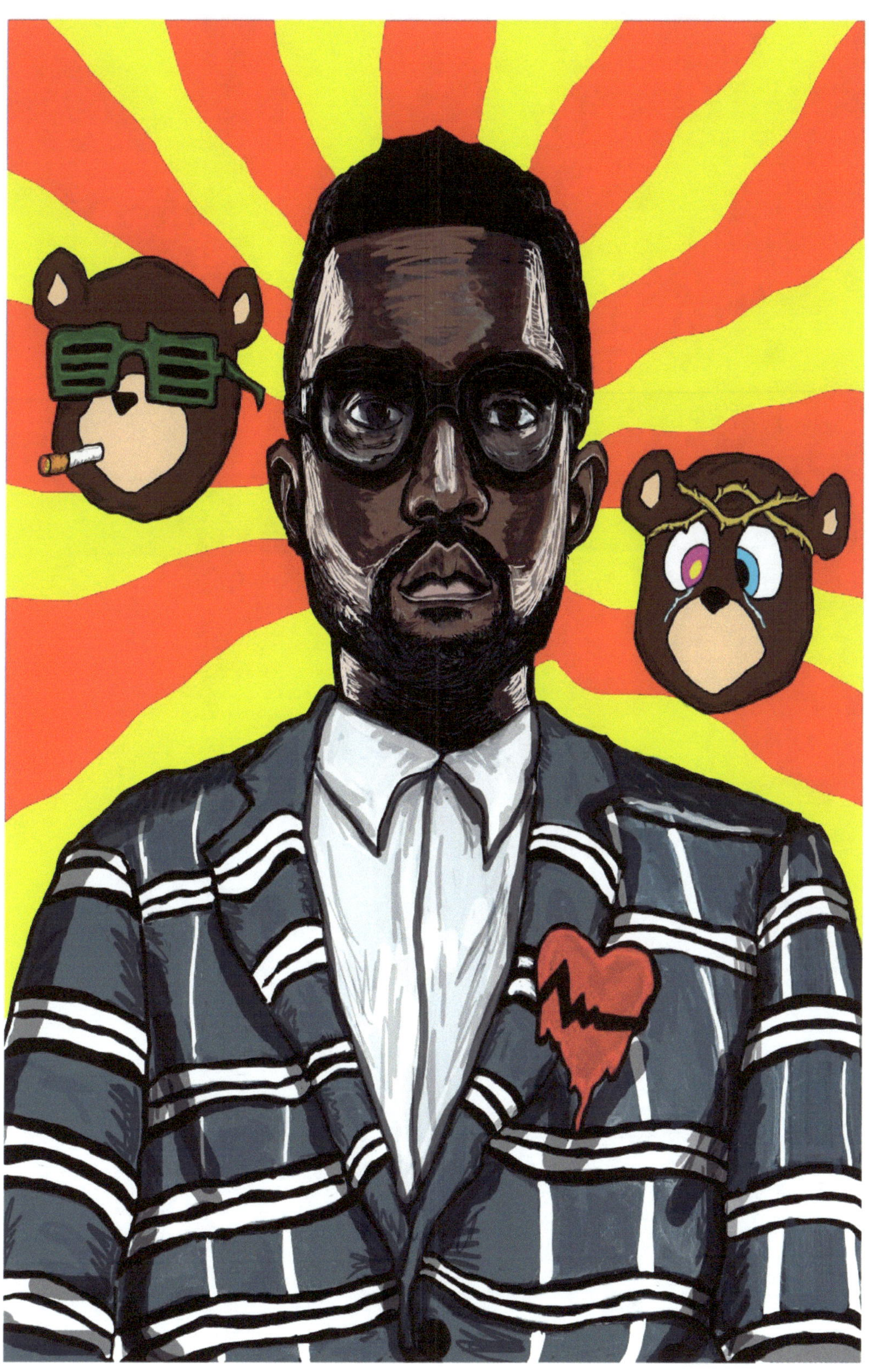

"Kanye West Portrait" **(2016)**

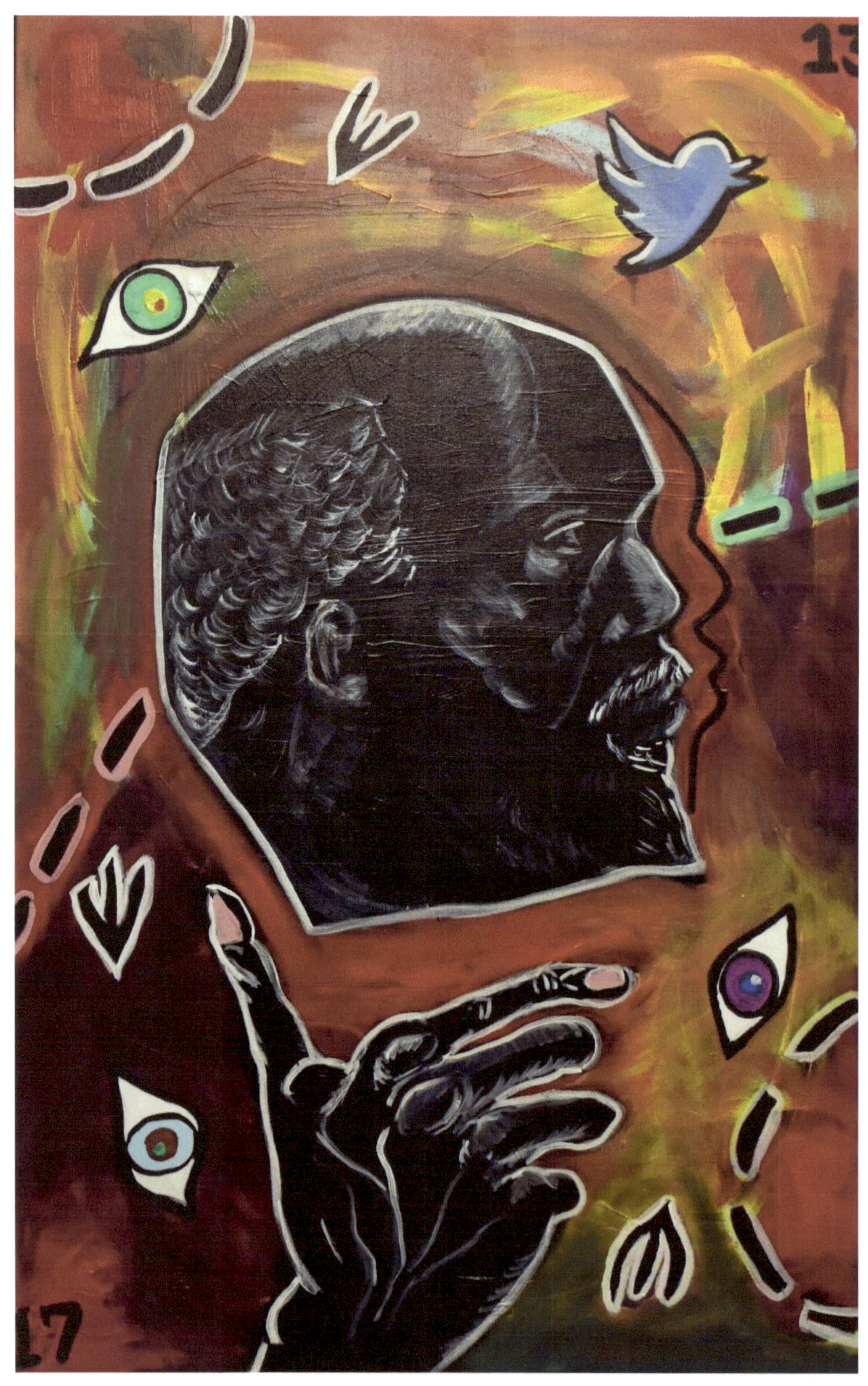

"Woke" **(2017)**

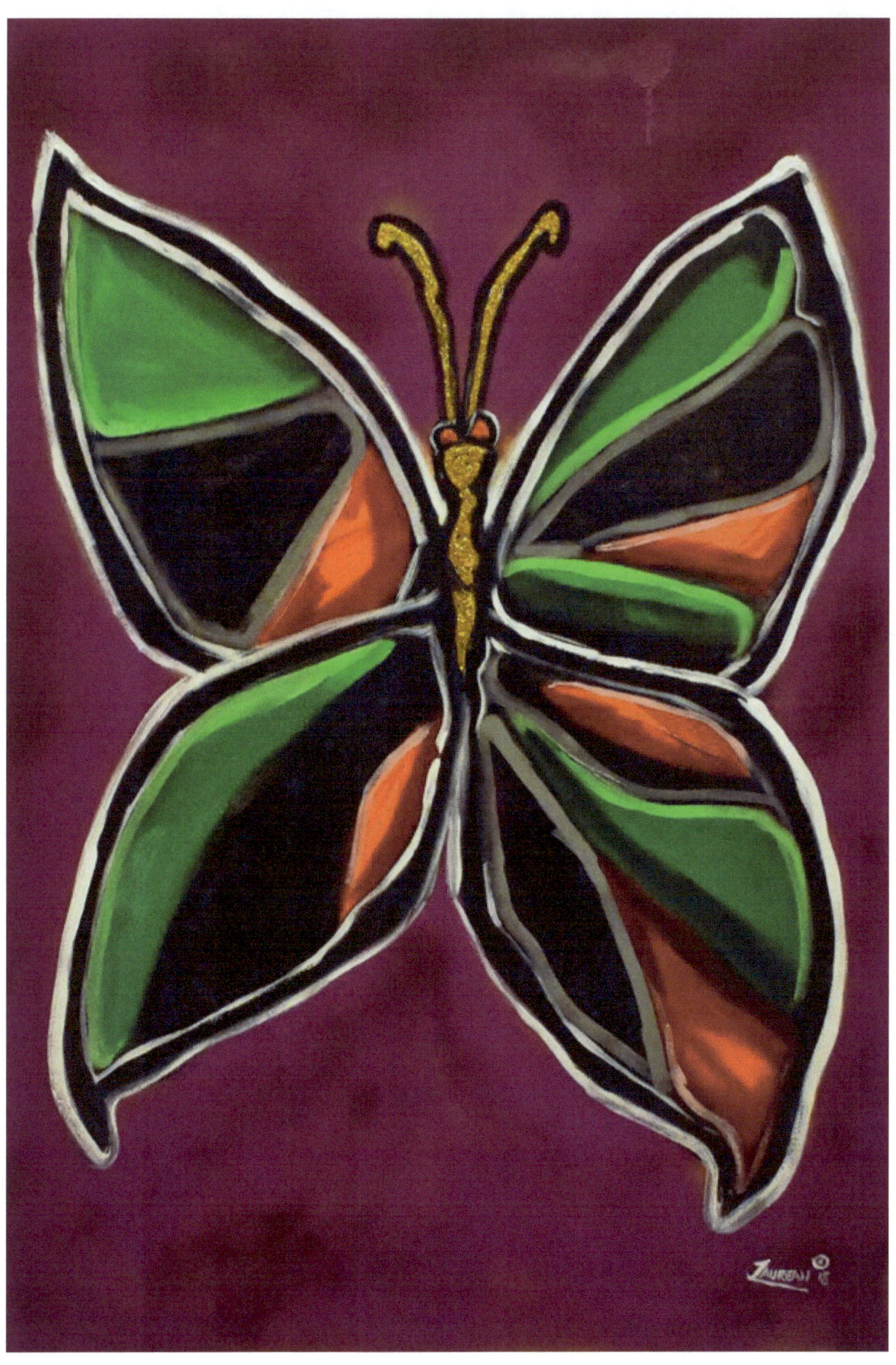

"Black Butterfly" **(2018)**

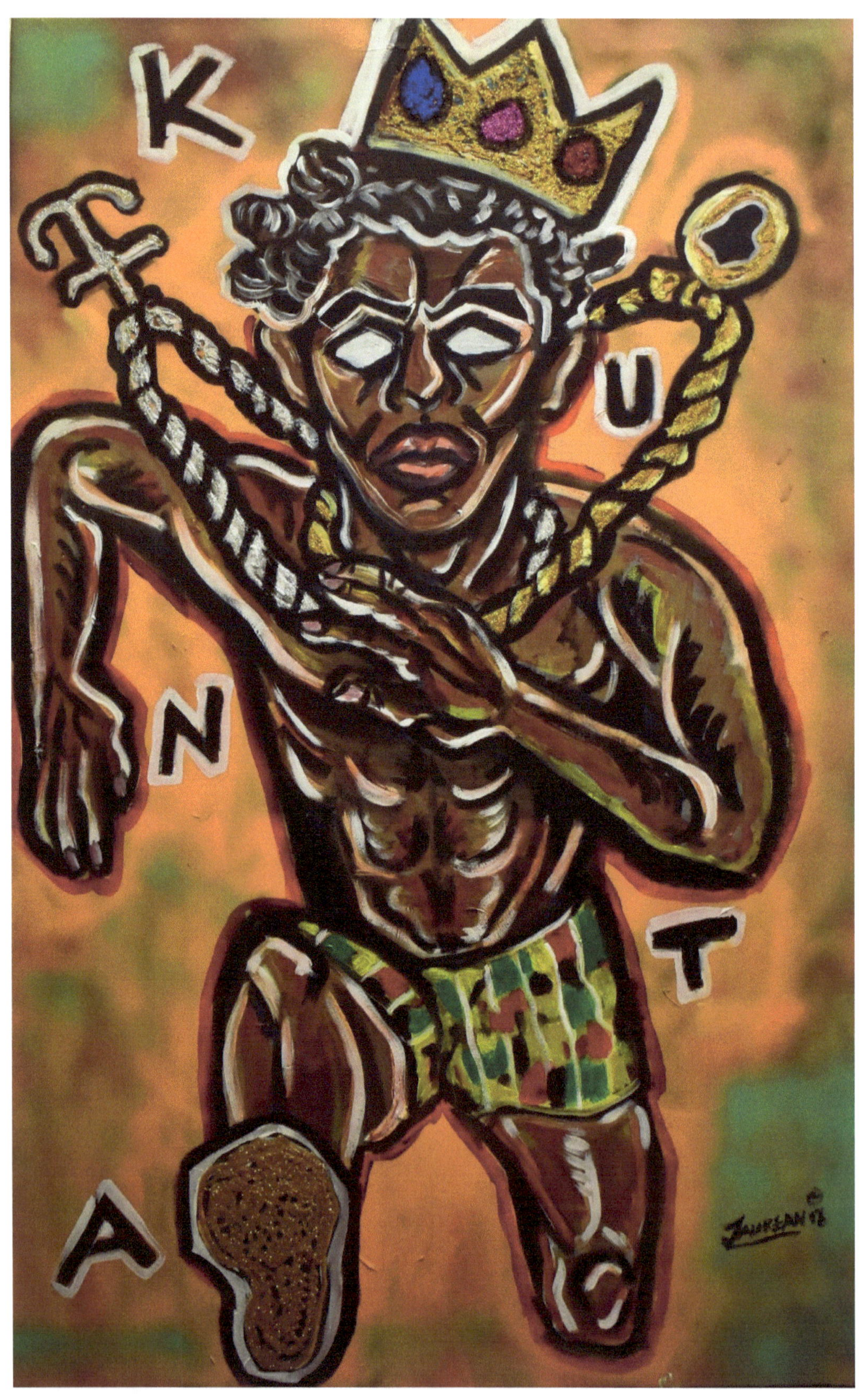

"King Kunta" **(2018)**

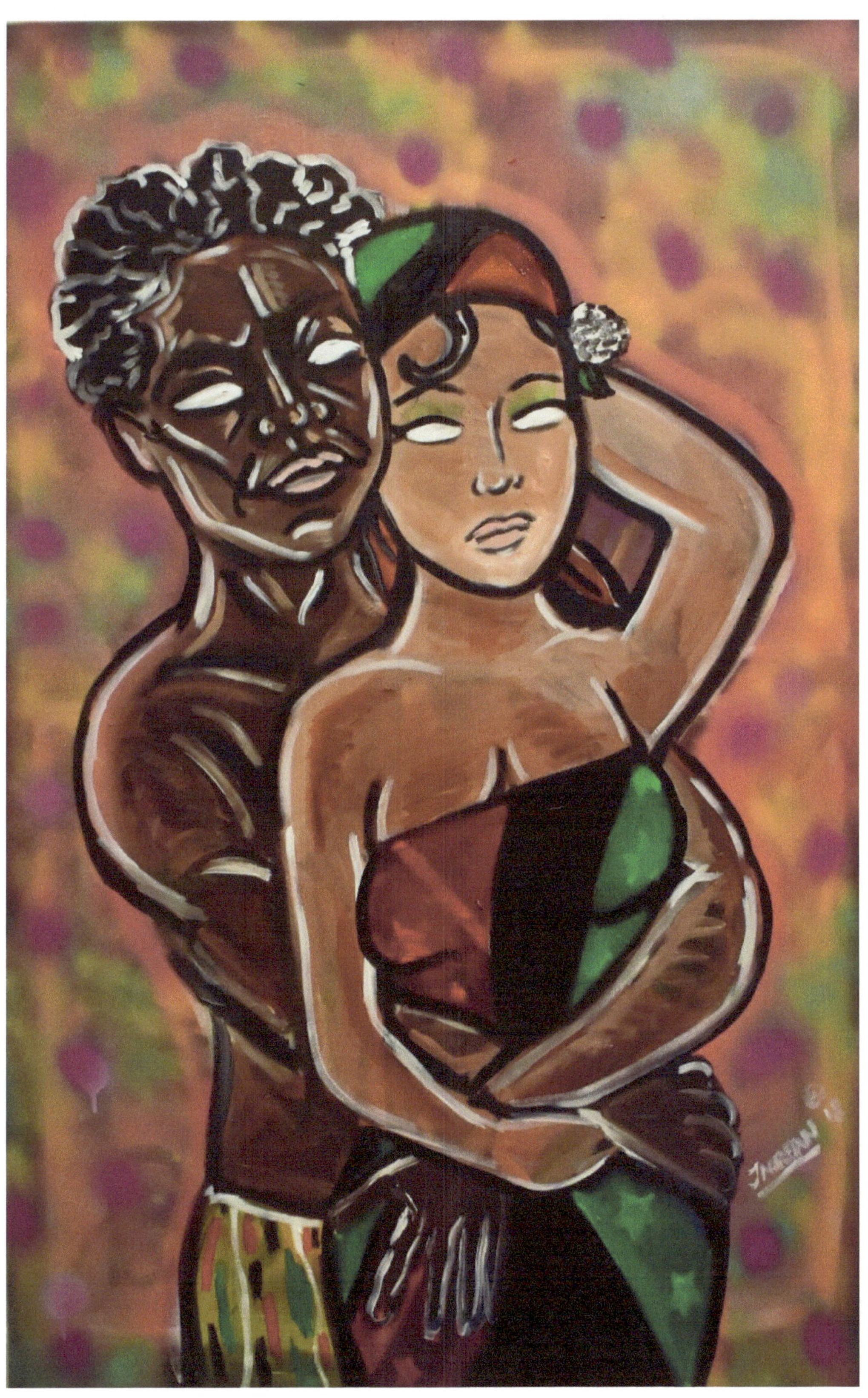

"Shades of Love" **(2018)**

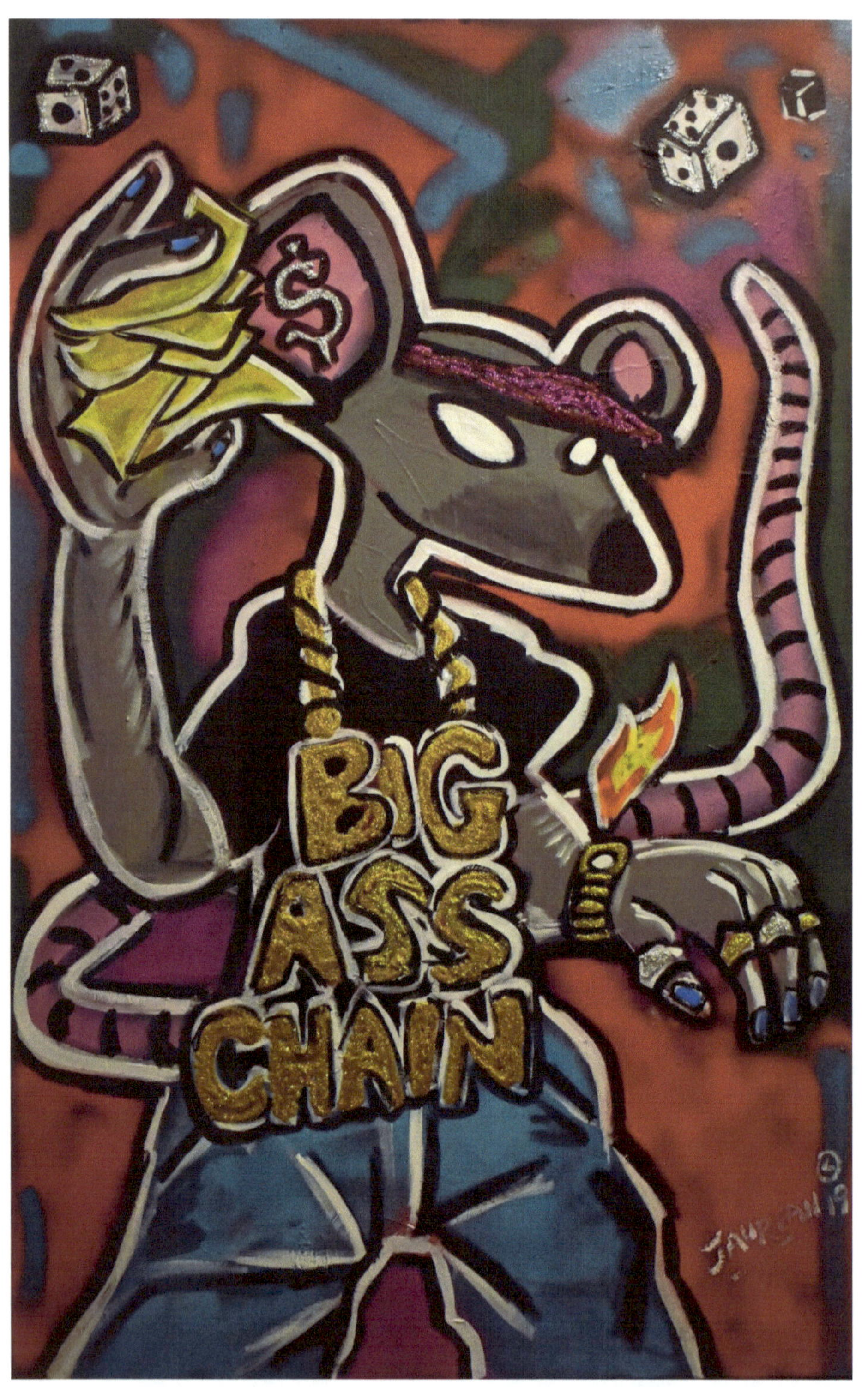

"Scorched Rollie" (**2019**)

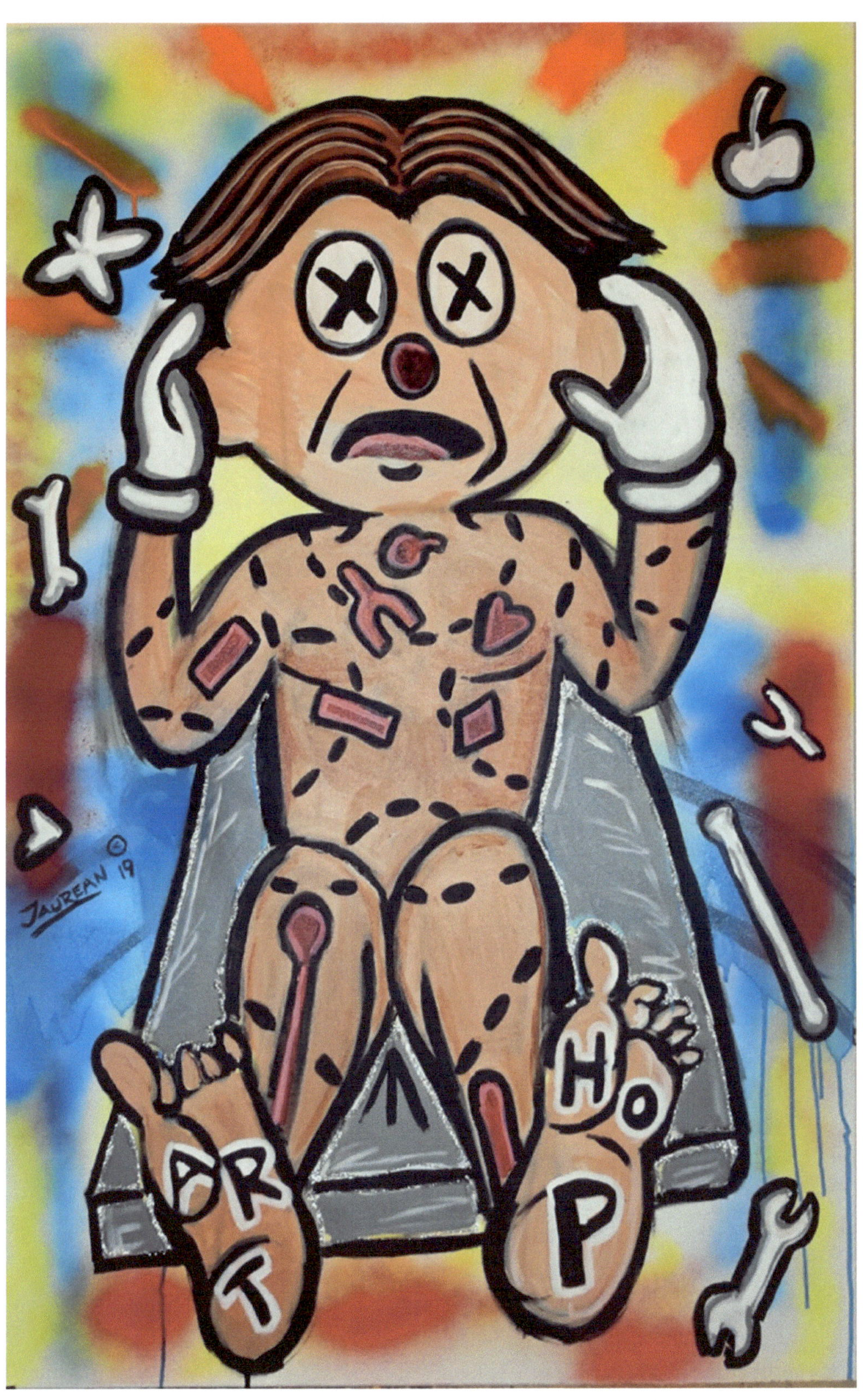

"Dr. Carter's Patient" **(2019)**

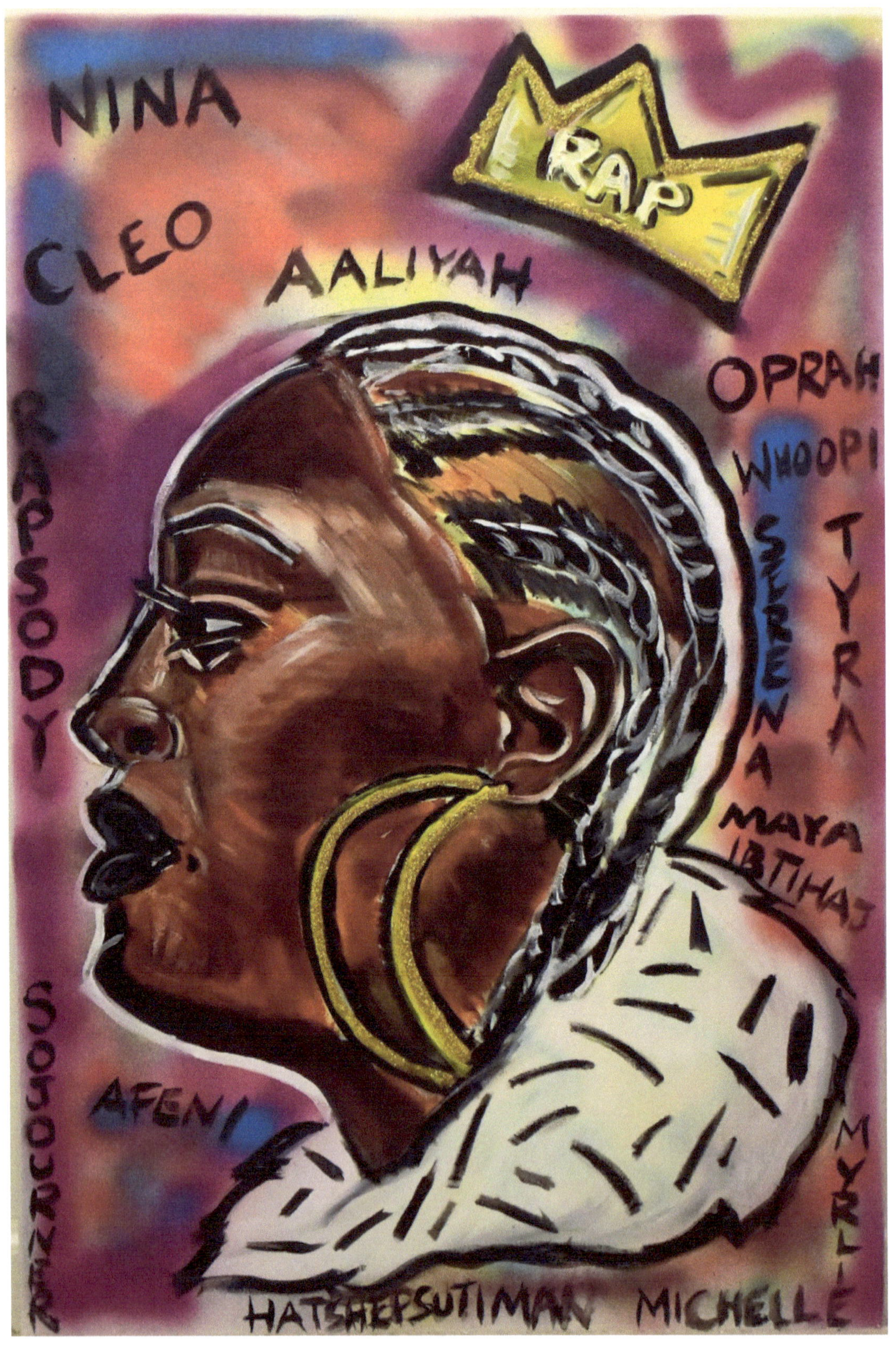

"Portrait of Rap" **(2019)** *Note to Rapsody, you are top 5 and can't wait for your album

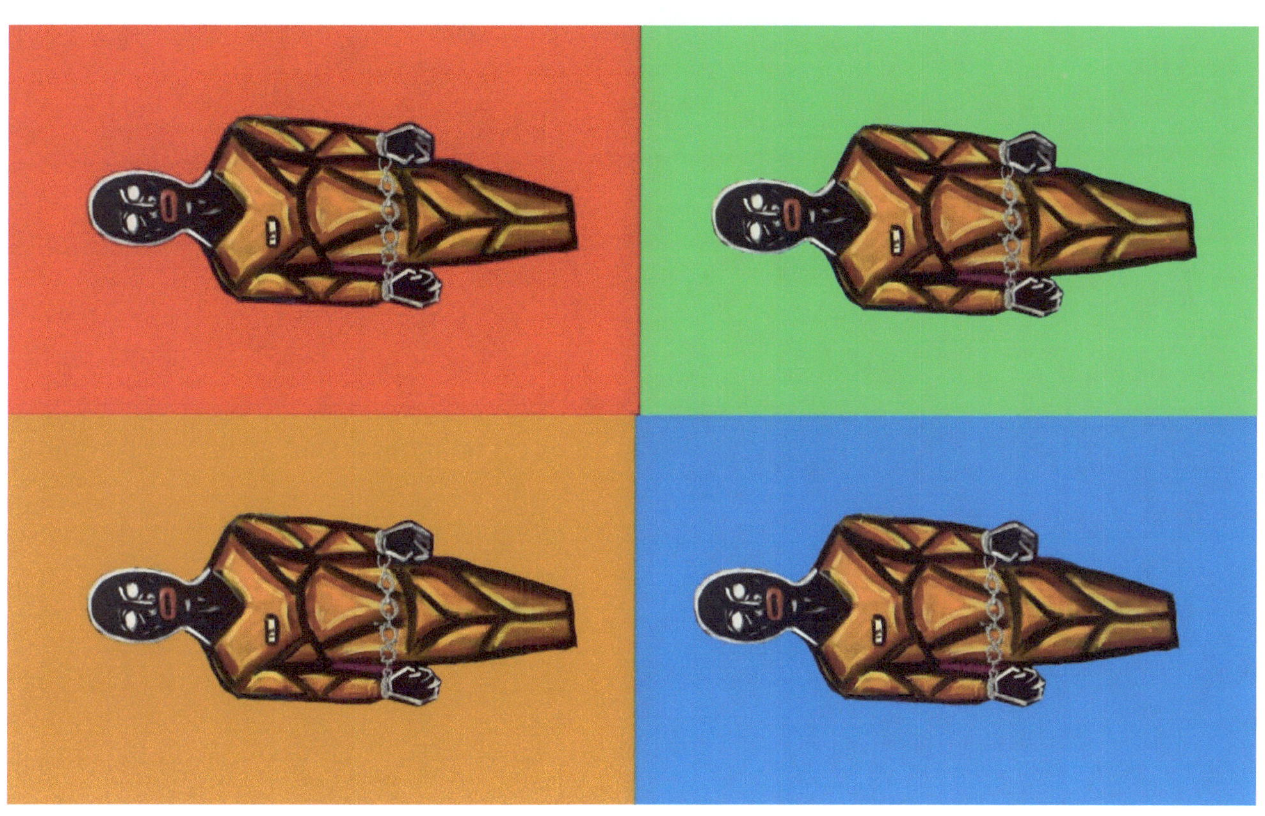

"POP-ulation Control" **(2020)**

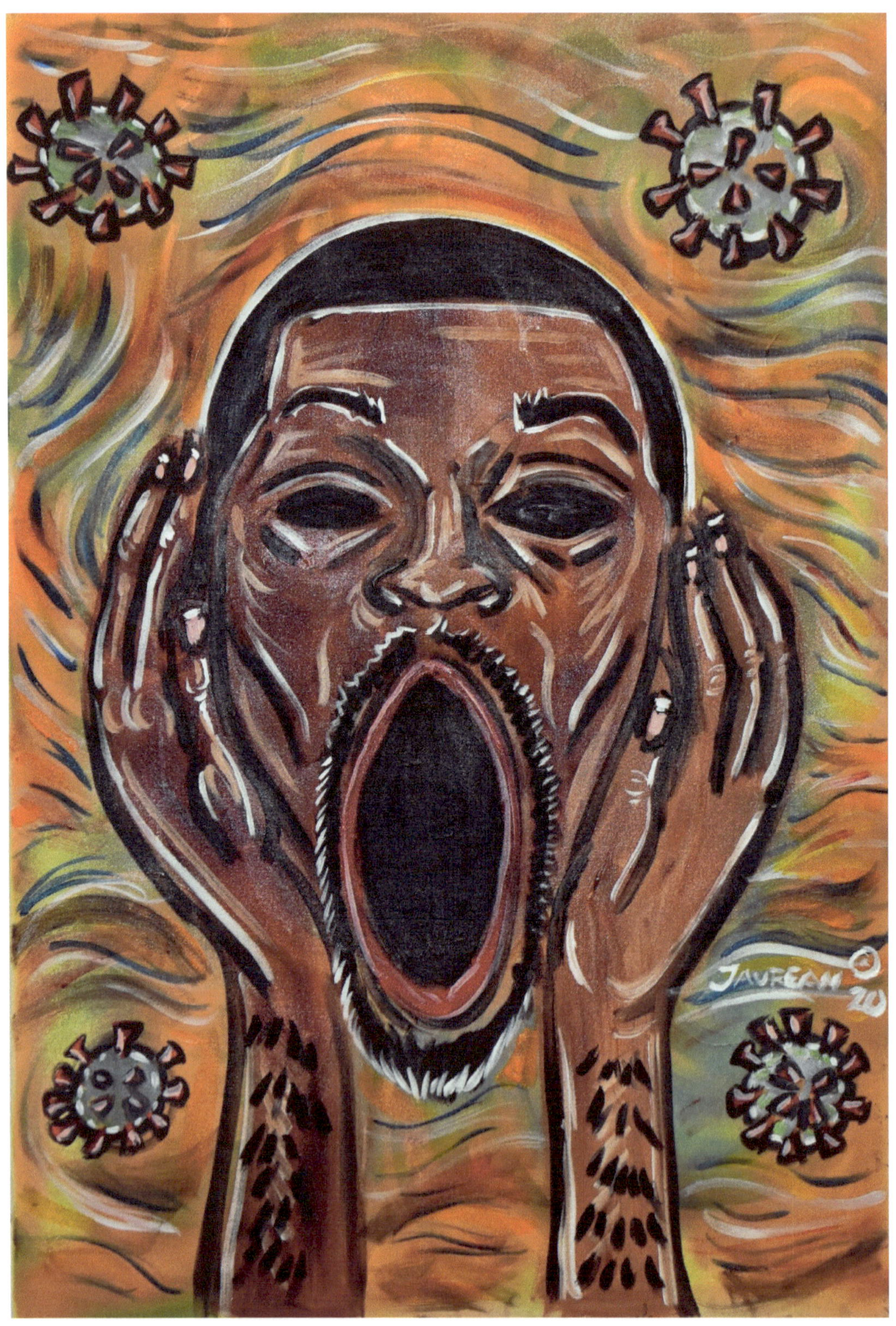

"The Corona Scream" **(2020)**

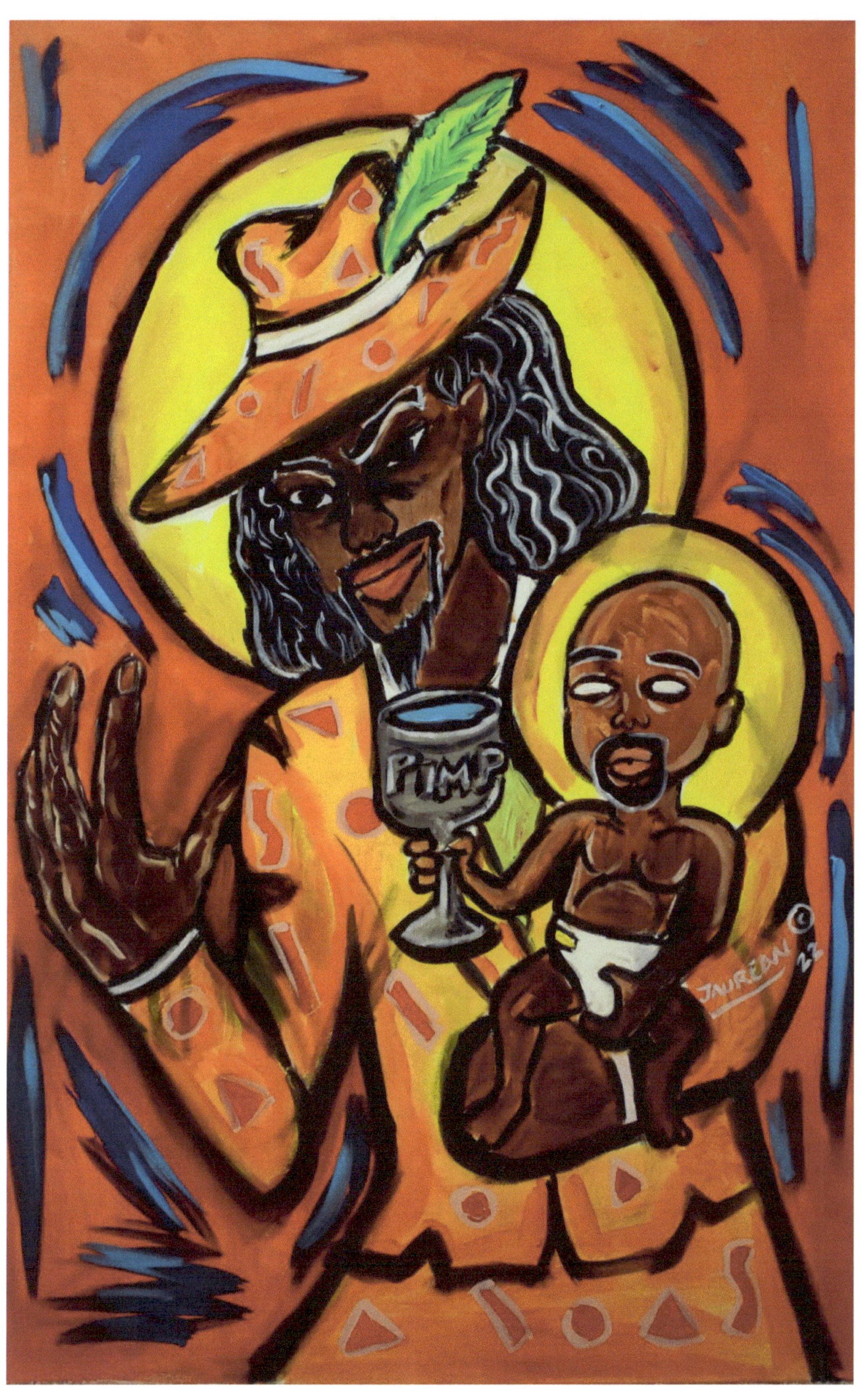

"Like Father, Like Son" **(20220** *Derived from my personal life, will share with you in due time

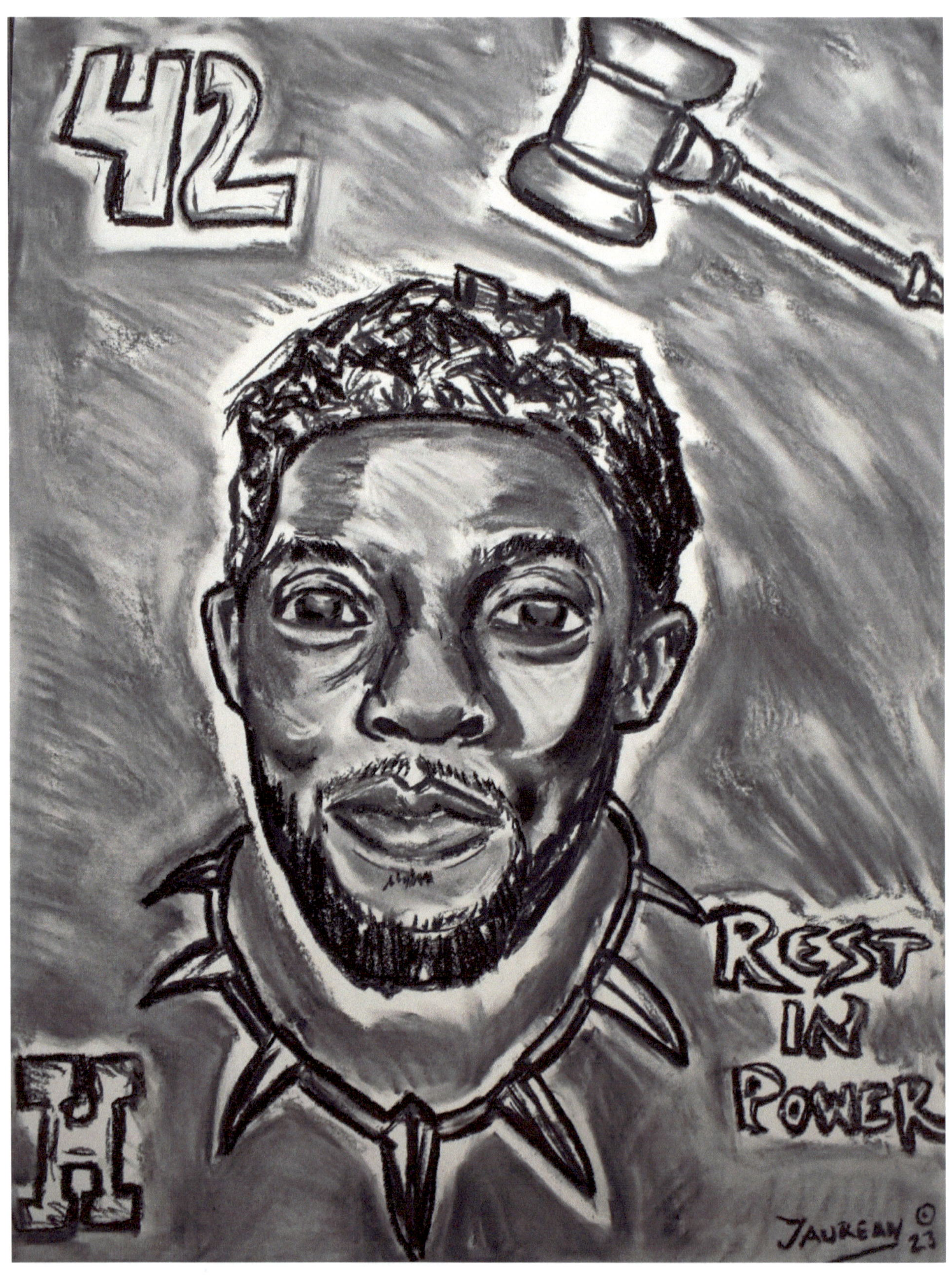

"Chadwick Boseman" **(2023)** *Rest in peace King

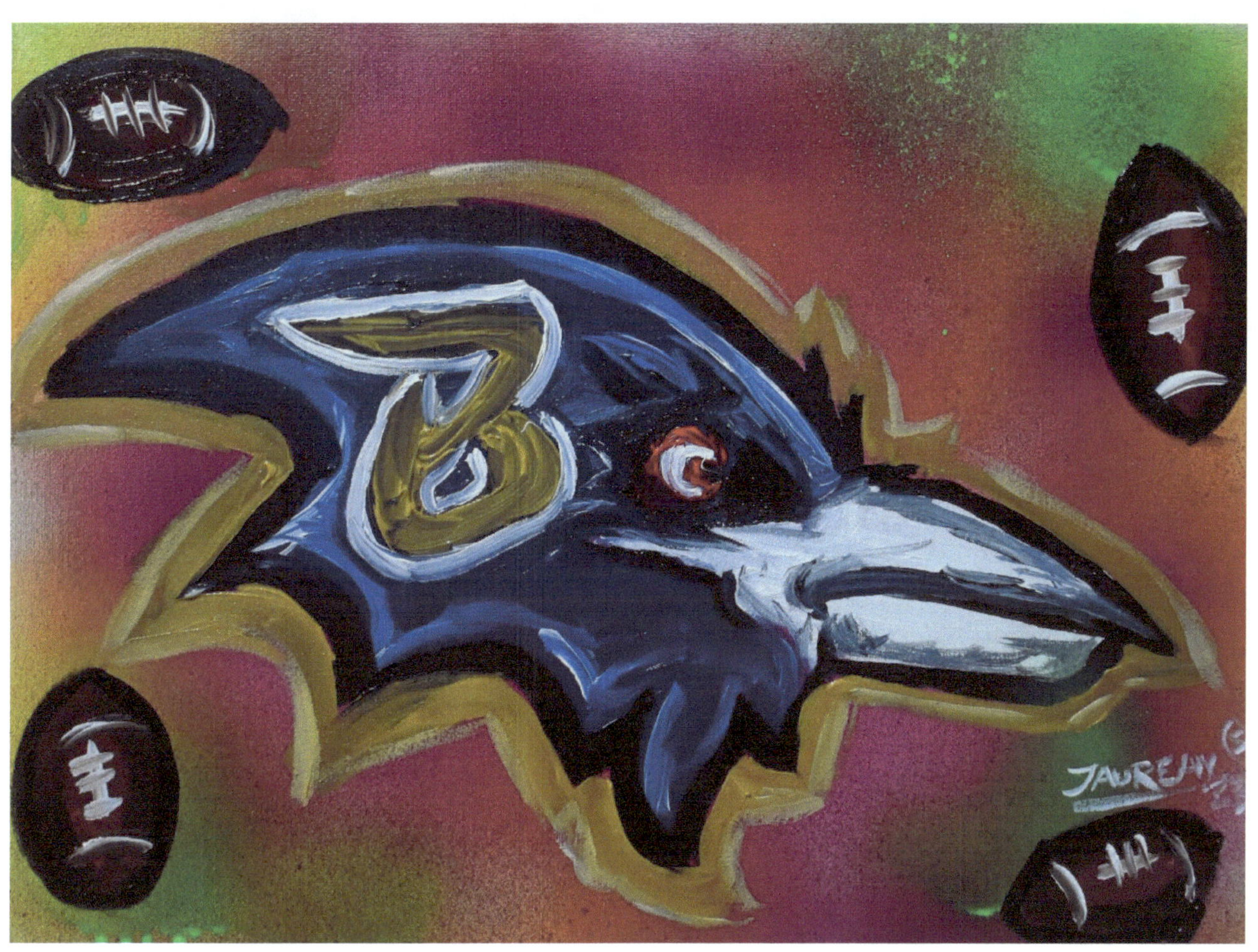

"Raven Bout it" **(2023)** *Let's go Ravens!!! #Ravens Flock

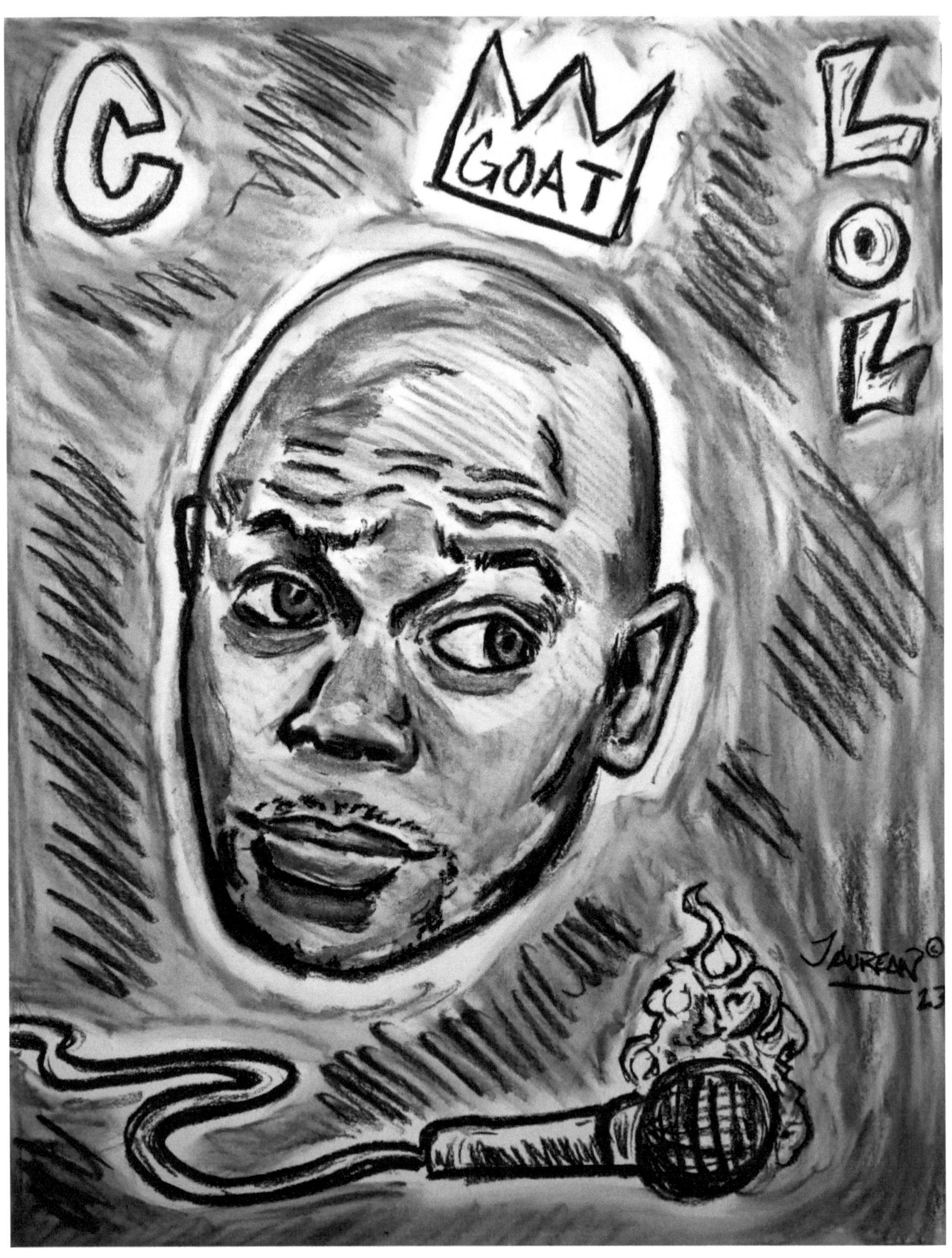

"Dave Chapelle" **(2023)**

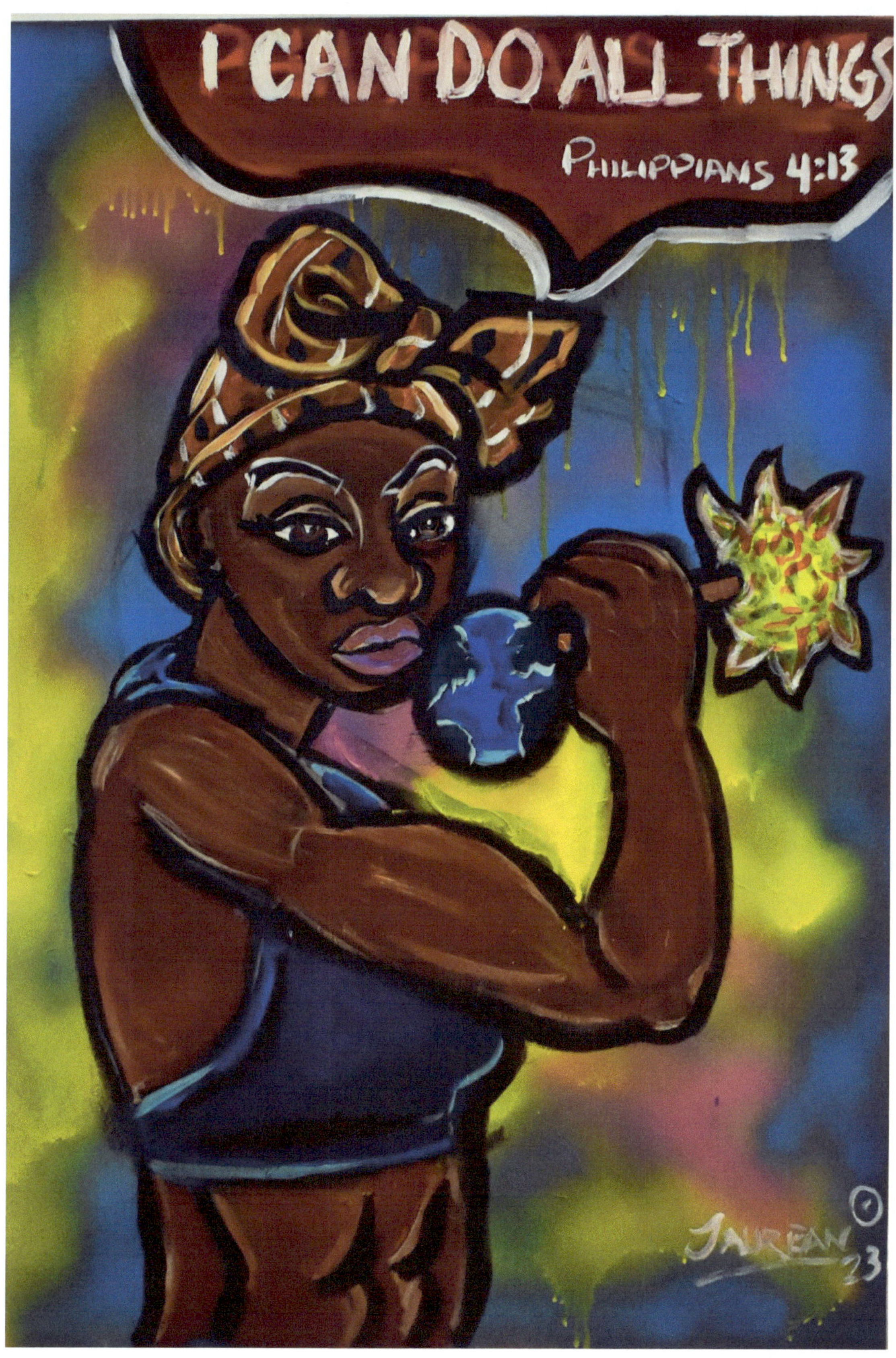

"I Can Do All Things" **(2023)** *None of this is possible without GOD Period! To HIM the Glory

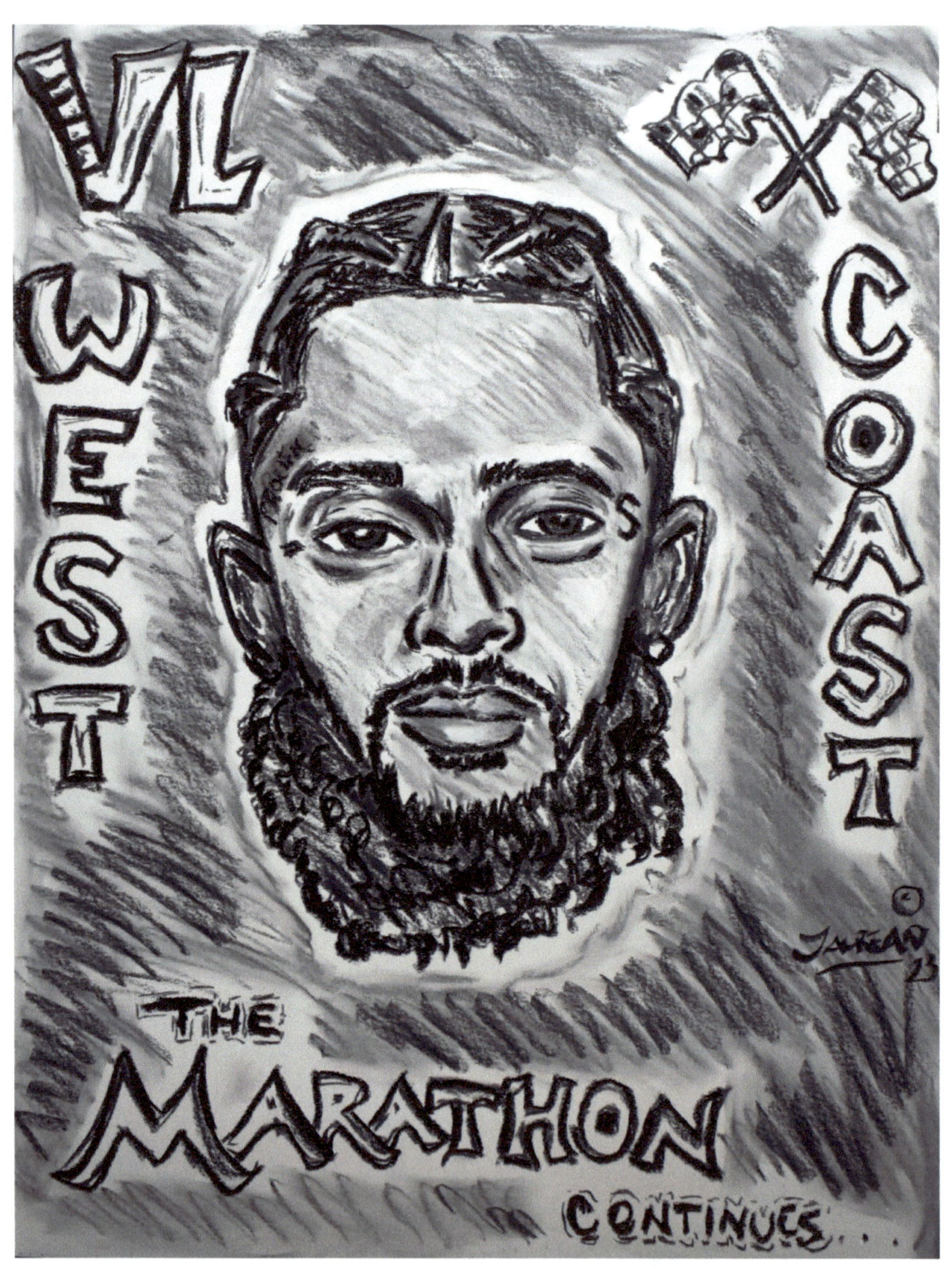

"Nipsey Hustle" **(2023)** *Thank you so much for the inspiration, I took some jewels and I got it!

HALFTIME

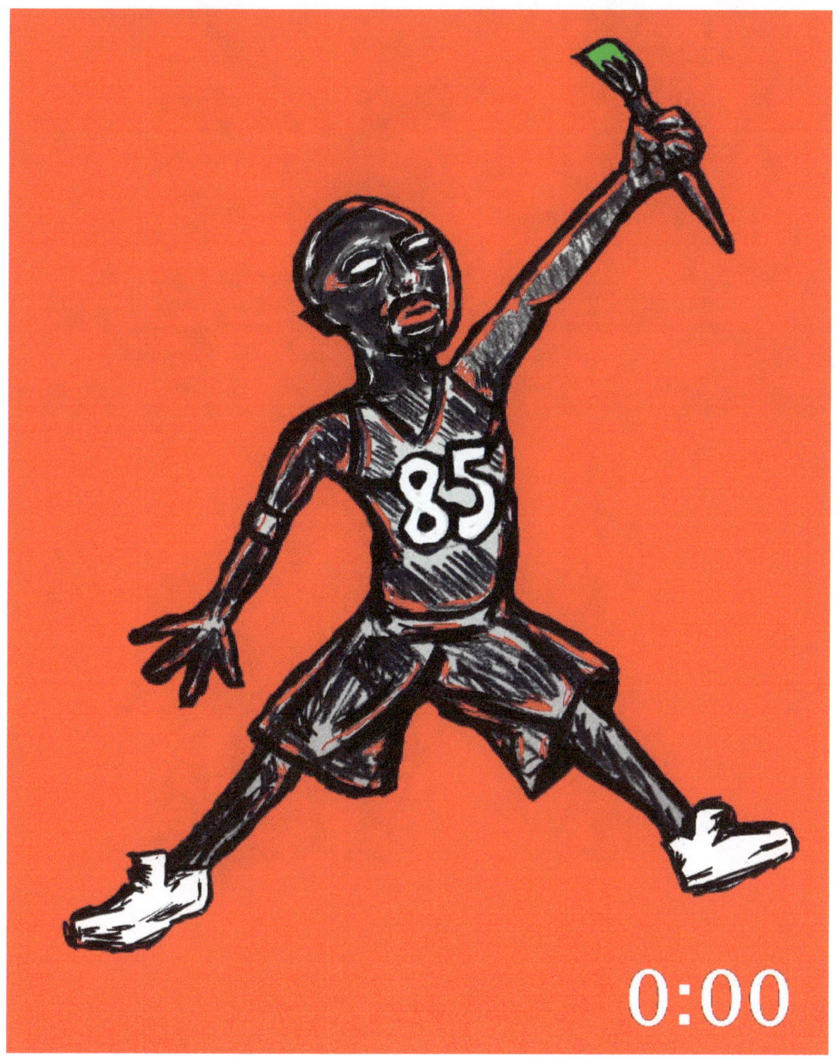

With that, that is the end of half time........Oh what a minute! I think I need to give you a little preview of what is coming next quarter so the competition knows what is in store! Check out ya boy at work! I'm cooking like Steph Curry with the brush!

BONUS:

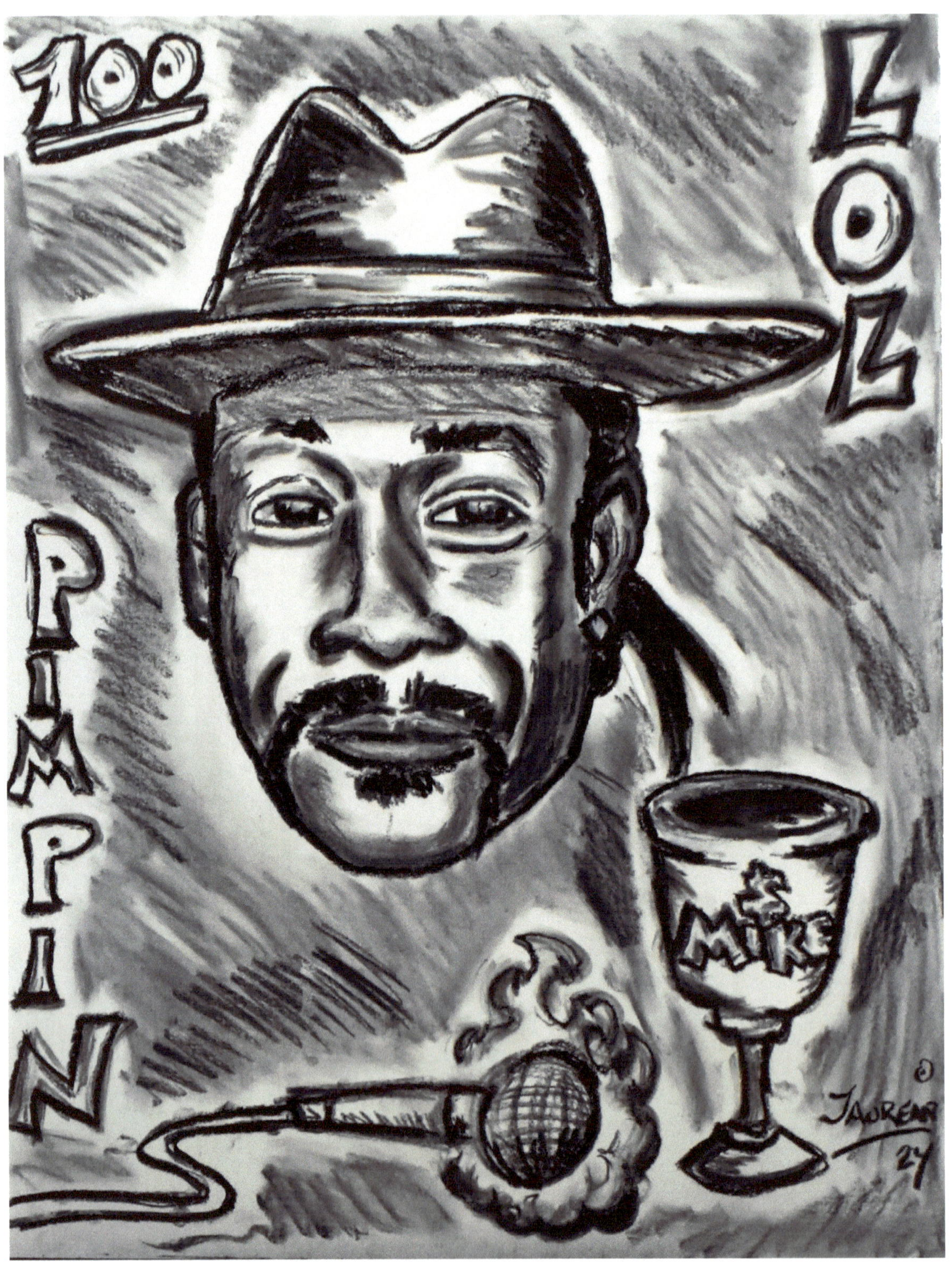

"Katt Williams" (**2024**) *You set the world on fire so far in 2024! LOL

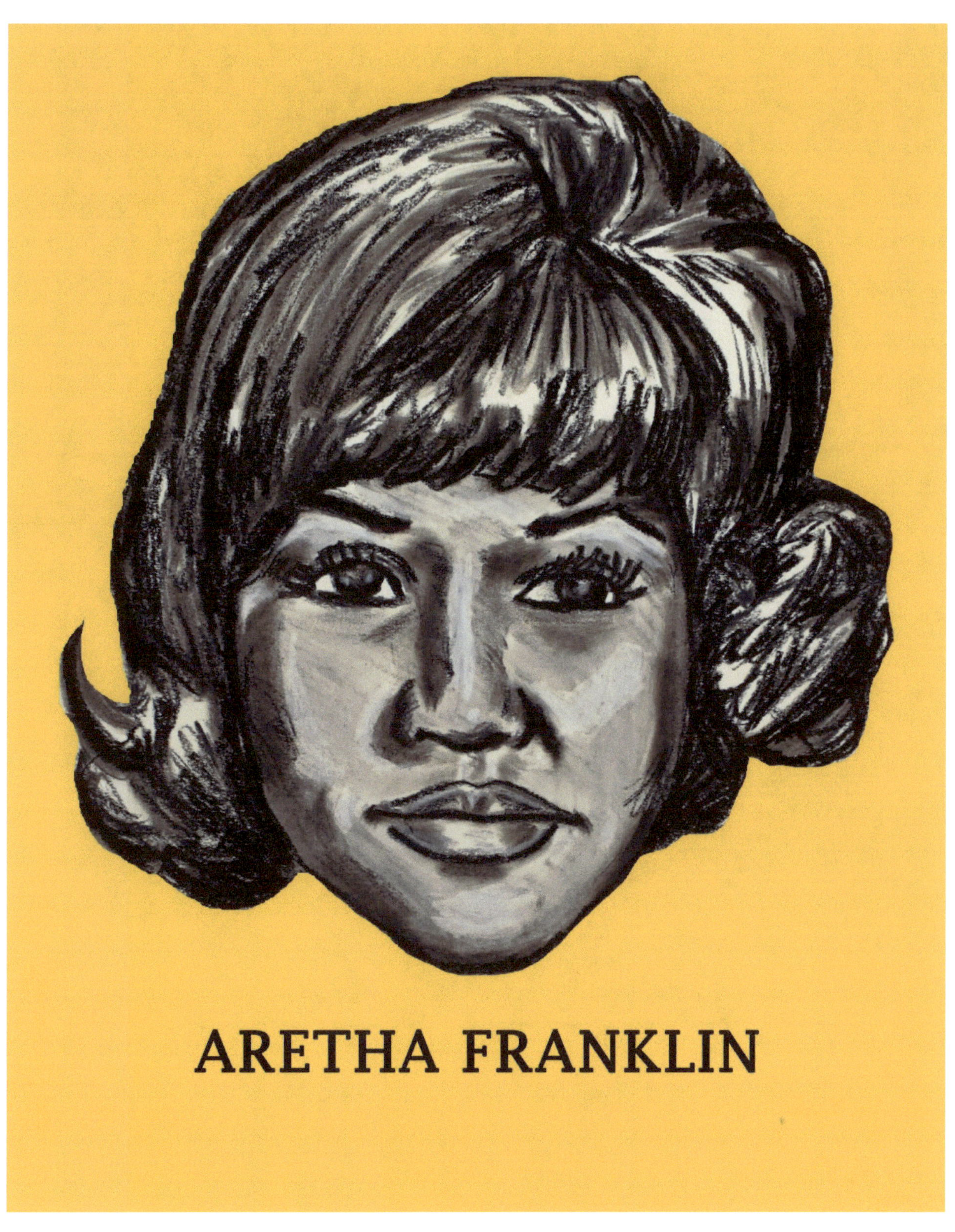

"Aretha Franklin" (2024) ***Rest in peace to the Queen of Soul"**

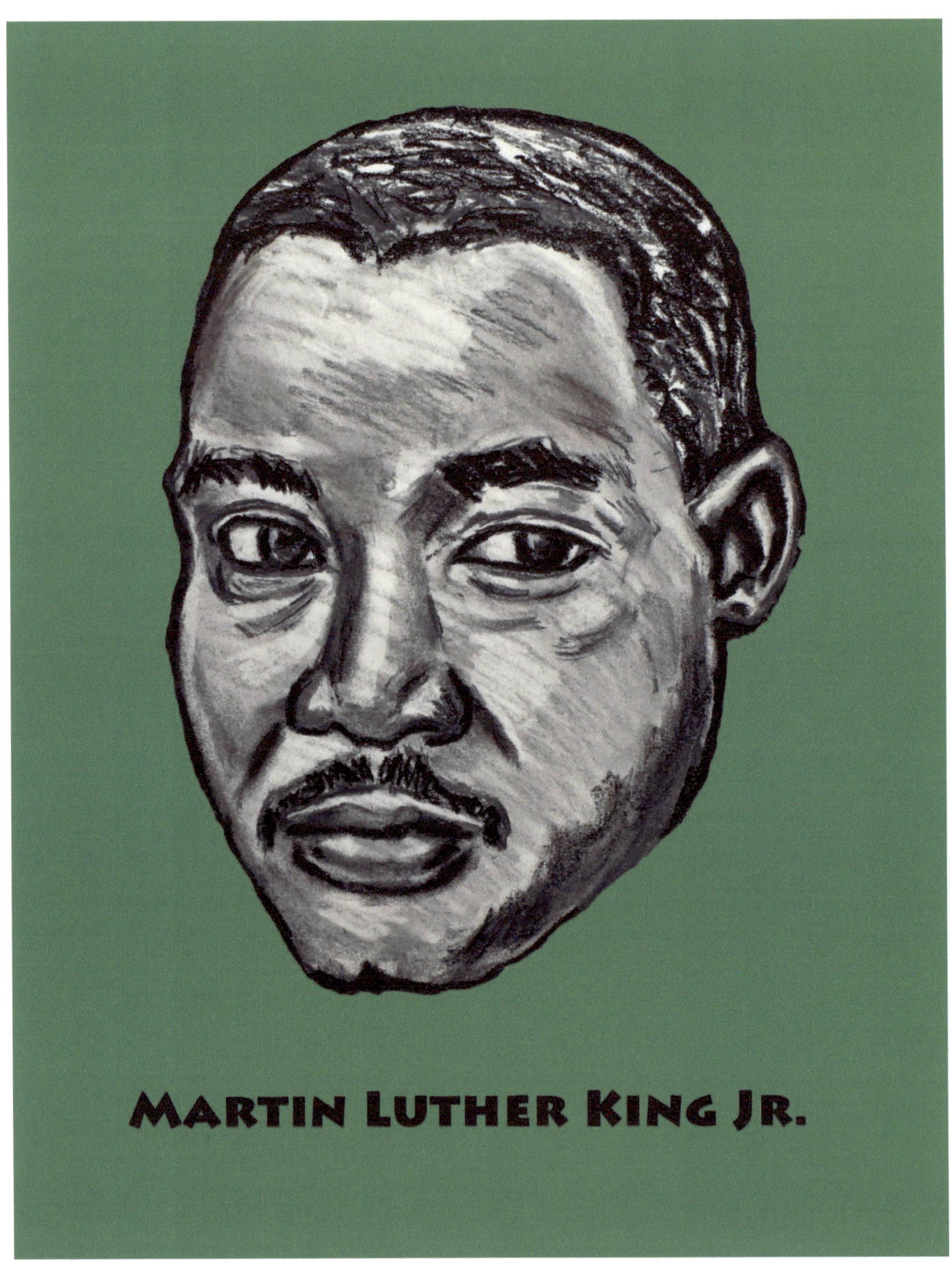

"Martin Luther King Jr." **(2024)** *Rest in Peace to amazing human

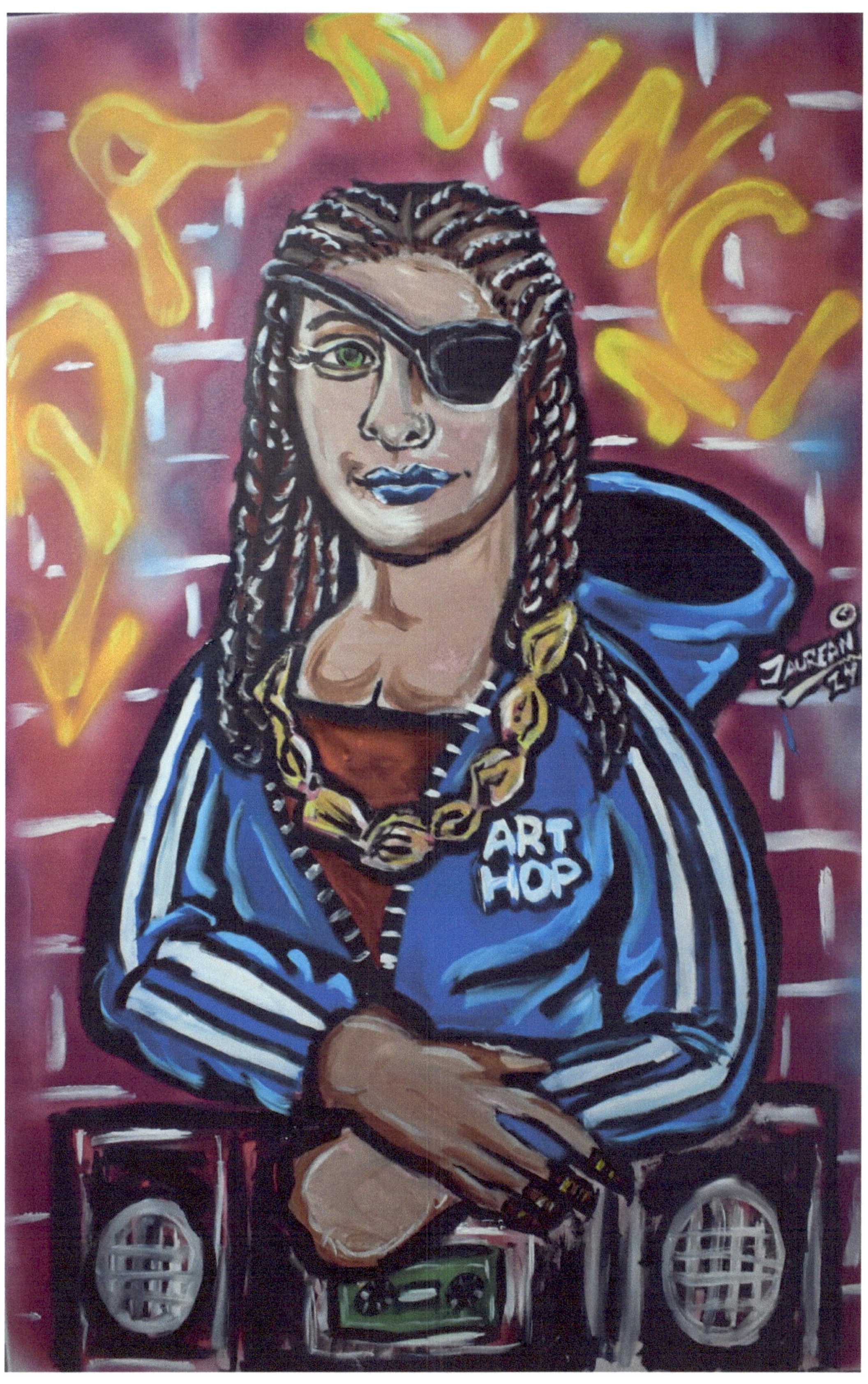

"Mona Lisa: The Remix" **(2024)** *Salute to Slick the Ruler-More info coming Jul 2024

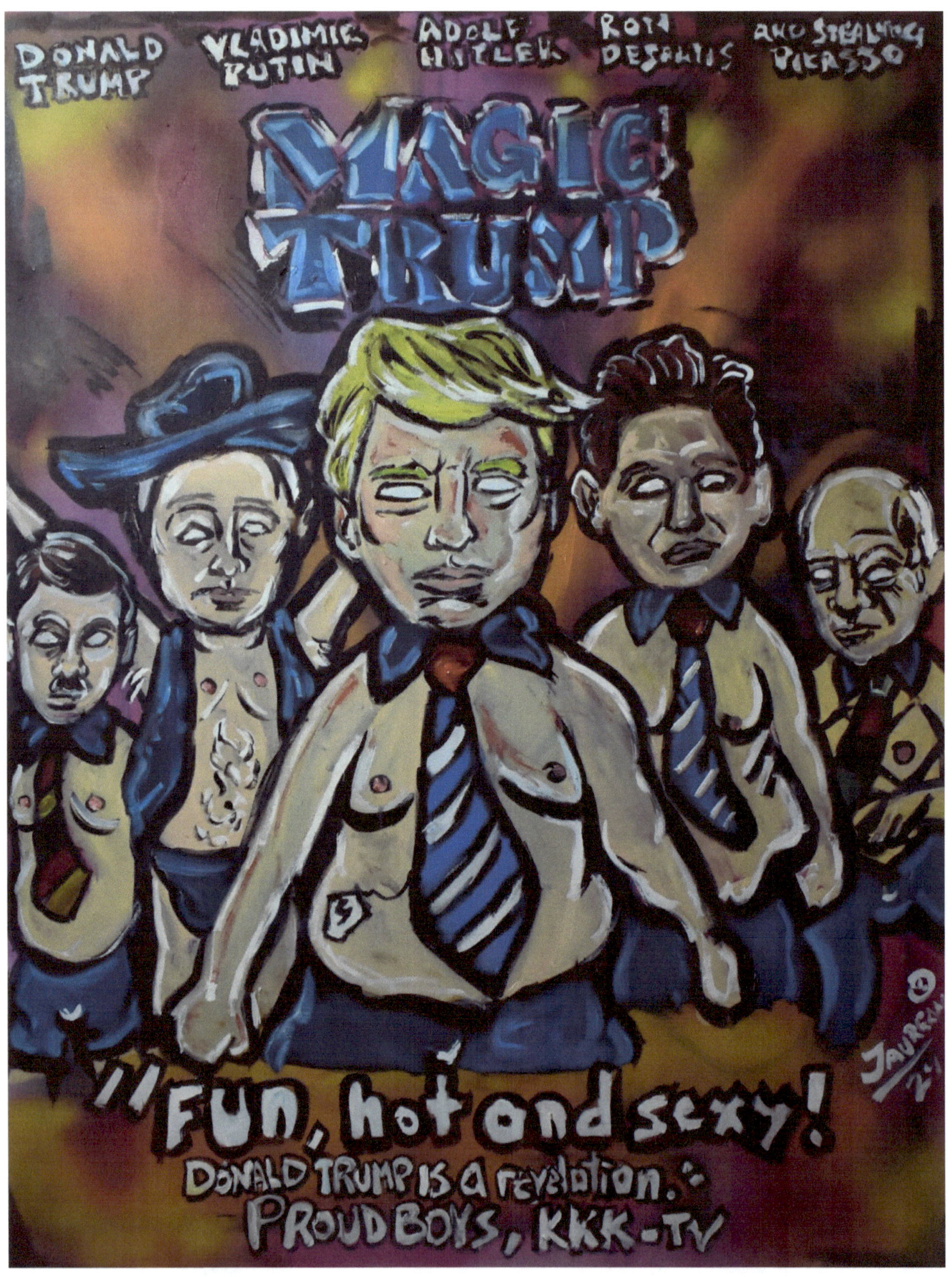

"Magic Trump" **(2024)** *Took a page from Picasso. I had to answer. Choose wisely at the Polls in 2024

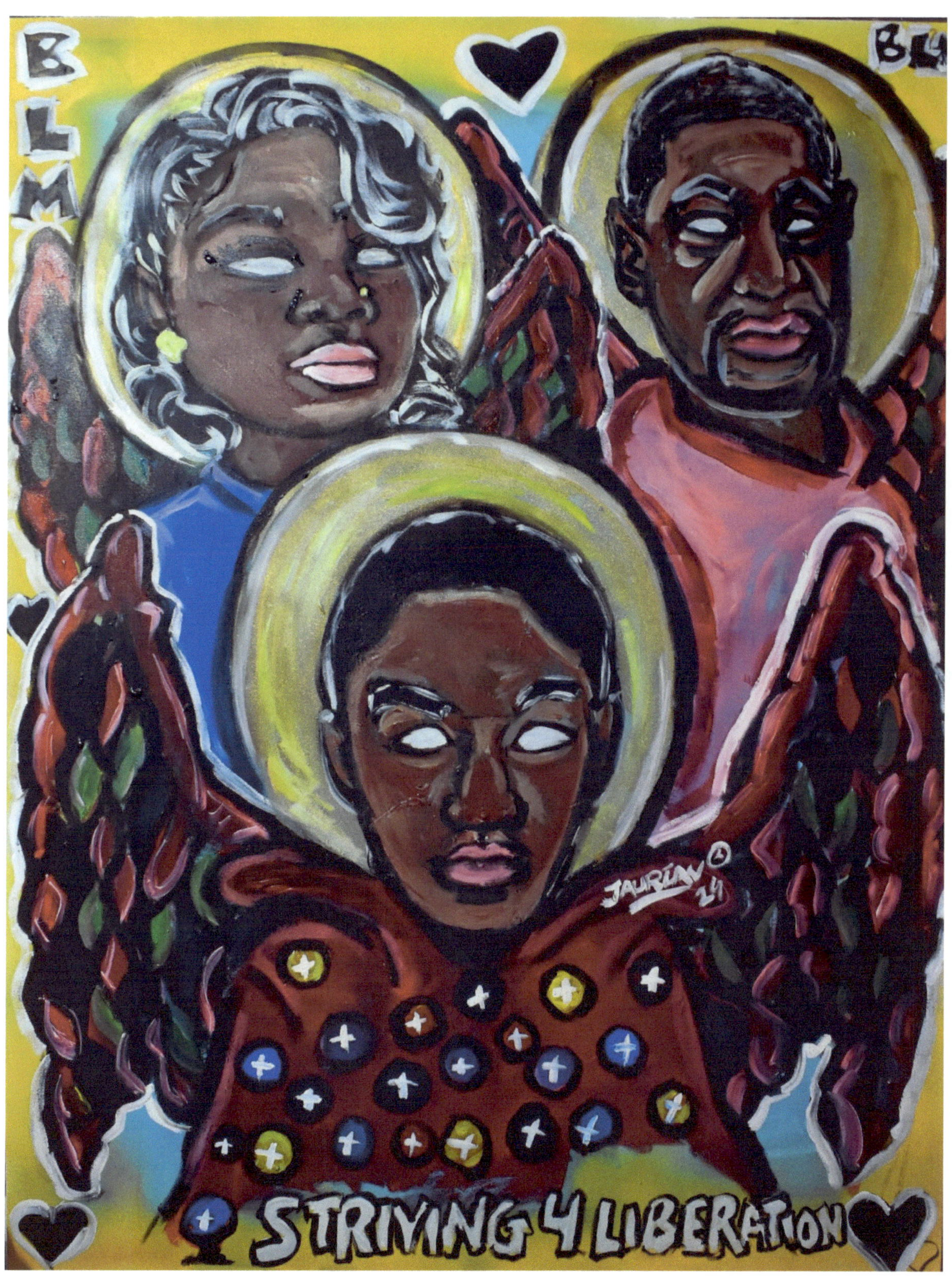

"Striving 4 Liberation" **(Dedication) (2024)** *This book is dedicated to the value and liberation of black lives

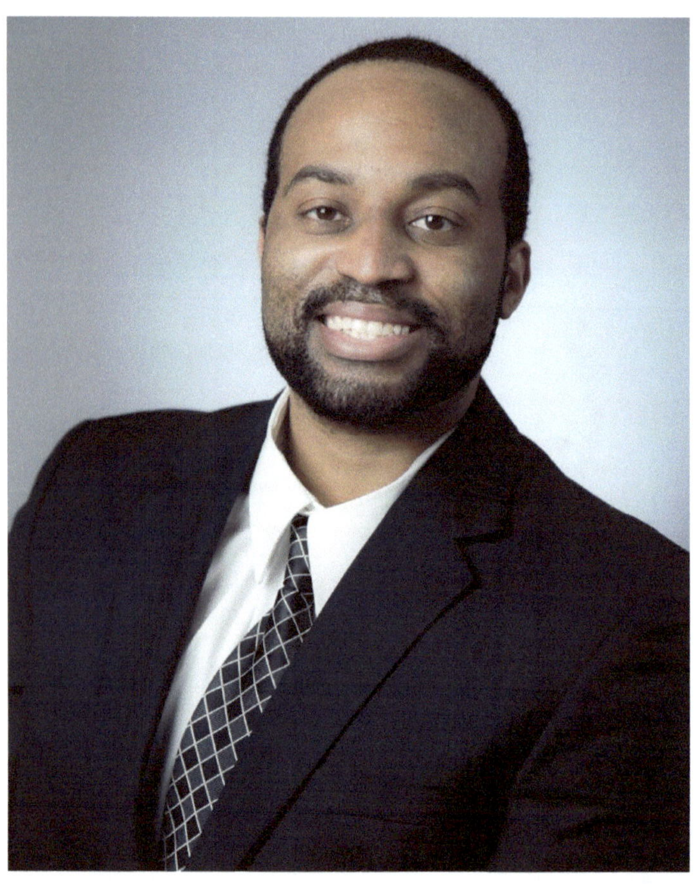

At Taurean Washington Studios we provide original art and art products to spread creativity to apply to your everyday lives. From art hanging in your home to art on the coffee mug you sip in the morning, we want to visually energize and provide a positive emotional impact to your life. Art is made from a place of service and intention to be inclusive of the underrepresented, marginalized, and overlooked. We want the 99% of our society to experience high quality art and know grow a new generation of collectors and lovers of art.

"As an African American who has emerged from minimum wage to earn six figures from my 9-5 and was on the longer route to achieve later success in life with my art and professional career, I was positioned against the grain to grab a slice of the American pie. With Taurean Washington Studios, we want to serve that slice of creative pie to anyone whether you are on minimum wage or you are in a great financial position in life."

-Taurean (join our tribe at **www.taureanwashingtonstudios.com**